Confessions of a Recovering Slut

ALSO BY HOLLIS GILLESPIE

Bleachy-Haired Honky Bitch:
Tales from a Bad
Neighborhood

Confessions of a Recovering Slut

AND OTHER LOVE STORIES

Hollis Gillespie

1Ю ReganBooks
Celebrating Ten Bestselling Years
An Imprint of HarperCollins*Publishers*

HarperCollins books may be purchased for educational, business, or sales promotional use. For information please write: Special Markets Department, HarperCollins Publishers Inc., 10 East 53rd Street, New York, NY 10022.

FIRST EDITION

Designed by Kate Nichols

Printed on acid-free paper

Library of Congress Cataloging-in-Publication Data

Gillespie, Hollis.
    Confessions of a recovering slut and other love stories / Hollis
Gillespie.—1st ed.
    p. cm.
    ISBN 0-06-056207-2 (acid-free paper)
    1. Gillespie, Hollis. 2. Journalists—United States—Biography.
I. Title: Half title : Confessions of a recovering slut. II. Title.

PN4874.G385A3 2005
070.92—dc22
[B]
                                                        2005046486

05   06   07   08   09   WBC/RRD   10   9   8   7   6   5   4   3   2   1

To my daughter on her thirtieth birthday

THIS BOOK IS THE SEQUEL to *Bleachy-Haired Honky Bitch: Tales from a Bad Neighborhood,* the success of which was such a surprise that I finally took back the Tiki glasses I stole from Trader Vic's two years ago because God knows I didn't want to get crapped on by the karma gods and interfere with whatever cosmic alignment had come to pass to bring me the blessing of a successful book.

As in *Bleachy*, the stories here are almost entirely true (barring hyperbole, conjecture, and the occasional hallucination), though they are presented in an order that favors story line over actual chronology. In some instances the names have been changed to protect the guilty (and one innocent)—though, as ever, most of the guilty have demanded their names appear in bold print and plan to post highway signs hoping to direct readers to their front doors.

I **BET THERE ARE BETTER WAYS** to test your boyfriend's affections than to fake like you're considering breast implants, but I was winging it, people. For one, this guy technically didn't consider himself my boyfriend, so that right there might have been my problem.

"I'm considering breast implants, what do you think?" I asked him, knowing full well I have never, not even for a nanosecond, considered puffing myself up like a blowfish. I was just grasping for compliments, expecting him to fawn all over the place about how my stupid ass is already perfectly fine, especially my tits, which are big enough.

Not huge, mind you. Let's get that straight, though sometimes when I put on my special Robo Bra, the kind that magically grabs fat from my ass and pushes it all the way around so it sits up under my chin, I must say I can fake people into thinking I have cleavage as big as the butt crack of a college freshman, but that is fairly seldom. When I remove that bra there are always big red half moons embedded beneath each boob thanks to the underwires, and there are not many occasions when such a result is worth the effort, though passing through security at the Frankfurt airport certainly qualifies. That bra always sets off bells like a four-alarm fire, which means I'm set to get felt up like a drunk coed at a frat bash. It's wonderful.

Anyway, here I am sitting across from this guy over spaghetti, probably with pesto in my teeth, blobbering on like the pathetic idiot who is providing him oceans of commitment-free sex that I am, trying to cop some compliments on top of what will hopefully be a free meal, and thankfully he looks up at me with worry.

"I had a friend who got implants, and they took forever to heal," he begins, launching into this long story about the sufferings of this poor girl. I was thinking, Wow, isn't that nice? He's *concerned* about me. Sadly, even though you might be sleeping with someone, concern isn't always evident. I once worked a flight where two first-class passengers who just met got drunk and ended up humping each other like fuck-crazed hounds right there in their seats, which is not at all something I'd recommend. Anyway, the plane was making a stop in Lexington, Kentucky, before continuing on to some other city, and damn if that man didn't get up and leave that poor passed-out lady lying there spread out like a TV dinner for all the other people to gawk at as they disembarked. Christ, he could have covered her up, I thought to myself as I covered her up. So you see? Concern, I tell you, is not always a given when a lonely woman reaches out for affection.

So there I was, a lonely woman reaching out for affection to this man who could not possibly have been a worse match for me. He was Catholic, for one, and I was raised by an atheist and a trailer salesman who, even though he was not atheist, didn't want his daughter getting a God habit that would require him to drive her to church, thereby cutting into his Sunday morning beer time at the local tavern.

Oddly, I recently graduated from a Catholic college, though I'd managed to do so without ever having set foot in its cathedral, which I hear was really nice. I remember people were always getting married in there, and I'd be bustling off to the financial aid office to stock up on all my soon-to-be-defaulted student loans when all of a sudden I'd have to dodge a crowd of people who looked to me to be dressed for a funeral until I saw the goddam eighties parade float that passed for a bride.

"Yippee for her," I always thought, because I had a lot of Catholic girlfriends and I know what they go through with all that fake sex until the wedding day, all those Indian burns on their pubic bones from the endless dry humping. "Forget *that*," I'd laugh at them. "I'll be over here having *real* sex with a soccer player on top of a running washing machine."

So other than that thin connection to Catholicism, this guy and I did not have a thing in common. For one, he actually told me that I should feel good because, of all the girls he was sleeping with, I was the only one he actually allowed in his bedroom, and that is not even the most pathetic part. The most pathetic part is this: I did feel good when he said that.

To top it off, here he was being all concerned about me, too, telling me about the horrors his friend had to endure with her own breast-implant fiasco. "I swear, she was bedridden for weeks," he continued, "and then, to make matters even worse, the implants were the wrong size. They weren't big enough, so she had to go *back* to the hospital and get them redone and go through it all over again."

Gosh, I sighed as he took my hand in his, he really cares for me. "So, in a nutshell," he finished, "if you're going to get implants, just make sure they're big enough."

LARY WANTS TO BE SAVED, which is news to me because I thought he was happy with his hell-bound self. "I thought you *wanted* to be left behind to battle the big lizards of Armageddon, or whatever," I say. I really don't know if there will be big lizards, I just remember hearing there'll be "hell on Earth" (like there isn't already).

"Not *saved* saved," Lary says, "but a *fake* salvation. I want to get on stage when the Benny Hinn convention comes back to town. I want him to slap me in the head so I can flop around."

Here I have to laugh, because Hinn's handlers are pretty picky about whom they put on stage. I mean, they bypass all the authentic wheelchair-bound sick people, like the lady with Lou Gehrig's disease hoping for a cure, and go straight to the vapid-faced bovines who would believe anything, it seems. Lary could not pull that off with his curly hair and hatchet face. His teeth are not sharpened, but look like they should be, and when he smiles at you you're immediately disquieted, wondering whether he just put poison in your coffee and he's looking forward to watching the results. In a crowd of Benny Hinn fanatics, Lary would stand out like a horny old uncle at a slumber party.

"You'd be so busted," I laugh. But Lary is adamant. "I can be possessed," he protests. "I can get that look in my eye, I can twitch," and here I have to agree with him, because I've seen Lary twitch. I have even seen him fake an epileptic fit just to scare off panhandlers approaching him on Peachtree Street. At first I thought it was a bit over the top, since just telling panhandlers "no" seems to work fine, but then I realized Lary likes scaring people, which is pretty much how Hinn and his coven keep their gravy boat afloat, by scaring people with threats of hell and devils who poke at you with their forked penises for all eternity. So, yes, Lary can twitch and he can get that look in his eye. Christ, who'd have thought Lary had qualities in common with members of the God squad? "In fact," Lary continues, "I think we all need to be saved together, as a unit."

He's talking about our friends Grant and Daniel and me, and of course I stop laughing. "No goddam *way* are you taking me to a revival circus!" I shriek. I went to one in high school once, and the experience was so painful it actually affected me physically. I'd been invited by someone from my sewing class, a fragile girl with a face like a pail of paste. The worst part was the speaking in tongues, which entailed, as far as I could tell, writhing at the foot of an icon and gibbering. When I got home that night my mother didn't even look up from her book. "How'd you like church?" she asked, and I could still hear her laughing as I shut the door to my room and fell face down on my bunk.

So, no, I am not willing to put myself through that again. I think Daniel would be on my side, too. He won't set foot in a church unless it's a famous European cathedral, and that's only because it's his practice to visit famous European cathedrals to drink shots of tequila in the very back pew. Sometimes, too, he likes to drive through my neighborhood and stop in front of small A.M.E. churches hoping to hear gospel music wafting to the street from the front door. Other than that, Daniel would not go to church even if his sweet Wal-Mart-greeter mother begged him from under her Sunday bonnet.

Grant, on the other hand, would definitely enjoy a fake salvation, probably because he's completely impervious to the real kind. That must be what he and Lary have in common. Me? I may be the daughter of a drunk and an atheist, but even so—even after the attack of the tongue-speaking God zombies—I think I still have some soil in me for the seed to be planted, and I think I need to be mindful about who tries to plant it there. After all, a fake salvation is only fake if you want it to be.

"I'm just curious, why do you think the four of us should hold hands and be saved as a unit?" I ask Lary. "So we can all go to heaven together?"

"Hell no," Lary answers. "It's so we can pull the others back if they start to lift away."

LARY IS NOT ALLOWED nice glasses at the Local anymore. Just for sitting next to him you'll get your wine served in a water cup, I swear, and Keiger, the owner, has even instructed the waitresses to keep count of those, because Lary is "out of control," he says. "He's stealing all my stuff."

I personally think all the glass-stealing started last April, when he showed up at the Local with the aim to help Grant bartend, only he set up camp next to the mechanical Jaeger dispenser like it was his own personal canteen instead. Since then Lary has figured he pretty much owns the place, or acts like he does anyway, while Keiger is left to keep count of what's missing after Lary leaves.

Lary insists he is accountable. He says he steals glasses from other bars and restaurants to replace the glasses he stole from the Local, and vice versa, so it all evens out. "I'm cross-pollinating," he says, except that now all the other bars are in for some crappy glassware, because Keiger is onto Lary's shit, and it's probably just a matter of time before the other bars are as well, as Lary does not even try to be subtle.

I don't know why Lary steals, but I suspect he genuinely thinks people will not miss what he takes. I myself stopped shoplifting at the age of five, after the second time I got caught. I'd gone into the Thrifty drugstore and commenced plucking earrings and other costume jewelry off the shelves and jamming them inside the folds of a rolled-up beach towel. But soon my bundle was so stuffed with stolen things it was the size of a mounted animal head and just as heavy, so it was inevitable, looking back, that a clerk would stop me.

He hiked up his trouser legs before kneeling down to look me in the eye. "Whatcha got rolled up in that towel?"

he asked, and I immediately affected such a great imitation of autism that to this day I wonder if, you know, it might be real. The clerk wisely decided not to push it and simply pointed his finger at me sternly. "I'm going to tell your father," he said, and that was all he needed to say.

I had never seen that man before, but in my five-year-old fake-autism head he very well could have hung out at the same bar my dad did every day, he could have been best buddies with my dad for all I knew, belting back dozens of beers in glasses that would probably stay unstolen. Maybe he had seen me in there playing air hockey with my sisters, maybe my dad had hooked his thumb in my direction and pointed me out to the guy, and now here I was in his store stealing things.

I lived a mile away and ran the whole way home, dropping my shoplifted booty along the way. I looked back and saw a pair of fluorescent go-go earrings in the gutter with the tag still attached, winking at me in the distance like two hot-pink turds. But I turned around and ploughed ahead. There was supposed to be a shortcut through the woods but I always got lost when I tried to take it, and this time was no exception. I couldn't even backtrack to follow the trail of price tags I'd left in my wake because, believe me, new stuff laying around on the ground unclaimed doesn't stay that way long.

So I simply hurled myself onto a hillock and lay there unclaimed myself, praying to a God I only knew from what my brother had told me one day when he pointed to the sky and said, "See that giant eye? That's God." I did not see an eye, but I did see some storm clouds with an opening in them that was eye*like*. So I lay there praying to this eyelike opening whose memory, because it was a clear day, I had to muster in my five-year-old fake-autism head.

I prayed that my father would never find out that I had stolen things, because even though my mother was a major klepto and our house was full of stolen things, I knew my father drowned in his anguish over his own limits every day and wished better for me. I swore to the eyelike opening that I'd never steal again if only my father never discovered I'd stolen at all.

When I finally walked through the door of our house, my dad was in the kitchen making a cake (a *cake!*) and to this day I believe I blew my wad with God on that first go. When my father turned toward me I thought he was gonna beat me with the lid of the tin flour canister—because God knew he beat us with that thing so many times it was now so dented it could hardly serve its normal purpose—but instead my father, who had not yet had that many beers, hiked his trouser legs up just like the Thrifty drugstore clerk had done, knelt down, and hugged me hello. I'll always be grateful to God for that hug as well as those stolen moments in the kitchen afterward, when I thought my father would kill me and he baked me a cake instead.

ONLY WEAR PANTS ON planes, never a skirt, because the last thing I want is the plane to crash and cause me to end up rumpled on the ground; dead with my skirt over my head. I also fear all the falling involved. I seriously hate the idea of landing on people, or ending up impaled on a piece of freestanding community art.

Recently I totally forgot my pants-only policy because earlier I'd been stupidly hopping on Harleys outside a beach bar down in St. Augustine—and I say stupidly because I was warned not to by all the bikers who could see in my eyes what I wanted to do. But I did it anyway because, I swear, most of those bikers are proctologists or something, who only take their Harleys out on Sundays and don't even drive them that fast. So I figured if a bunch of wobble-bellied family men could pretend to be bikers so could I, at least for a second while my friend took a picture. So I went skipping over there, and the first thing I did was fry the shit-eating fuck out of the inside of my shin on an exhaust pipe.

"I told you not to hop on that Harley," the biker said smugly. I would have hated his flat daiquiri-drinking ass but I was too busy pretending the burn didn't hurt, which was almost impossible because it was seriously the most painful injury this side of having Spanish inquisitors pour molten lead down your anal cavity. At the time it was all I could do to run to the restroom so I could scream and sob in relative solitude. Soon my lower shin blossomed with enough blisters and blood and general redness to merit amputation, if you ask me, but according to a bunch of idiot off-duty doctors in leather chaps, all I needed was an ice pack and more margaritas.

I had to fly to Berlin two days later and I completely

forgot about my whole pants-only policy due to this major flesh-eating leprosy of a burn on my leg. The last thing I needed was friction on it, so I just sprang off to work in my skirt like I had no idea I was inviting Murphy's Law to come shit on my head.

Once there I realized the plane home was bound to crash. How could it not? Here I was in a uniform *skirt*, breaking my own rule about being careful to make a benign corpse in the event of a crash so as not to attract media photographers, and I had to deal with the knowledge on the entire crew-bus ride back to the Berlin airport, that the cosmic crap shooter was gonna let the ball land on my number now that I was unprepared.

The plane, of course, was scheduled to be full. I don't know about you, but that's half my panic right there. I just want some privacy when I die. My father, as far as I know, died alone in an efficiency apartment across the street from the Los Angeles airport, where he'd moved after my mother left him and took us with her to San Diego. He sold used cars in a lot next to the tarmac, and I heard he'd been dating a stewardess. A nice old stewardess.

I hope that is true. I hope he was not totally alone when his heart gave out, because he did not die right away. His neighbors told us they could hear him crying, and I am guessing it was fear, because he must have known what was happening, and I'm hoping he had a nice old stewardess with him to hold his hand to help him face the fear. They are good at that. They hold my hand all the time.

They're used to it, as there are plenty of us flight attendants who are nervous to fly, especially these days, what with 9/11 sucking all the fun out of everything. I know one who won't take off without her jar of lucky plums right there with her in her jump seat, so it was nothing when I confessed to them my fear the plane was bound to crash because I forgot to wear pants. They didn't ridicule me as you might expect; instead they just eyed me levelly, drew the curtain across the back cross aisle, and one of them traded her pants for my skirt right there.

They remind me of mothers, which makes sense, because when I applied for this job one of them advised me the best way to get hired was to fake every characteristic of a codependent. "You gotta know the right way to take the blame for everything and apologize," she said. So sometimes I wonder if my own mother might have made a good flight attendant if her propensity for designing missiles hadn't panned out. I was always falling, it seemed, and my mother was always catching me, or she tried to, until the day came when she couldn't anymore. That's what parents do. They catch their kids when they fall.

Or they try to. And now I wish I could keep from thinking about this, because it makes the images of the parents looking for their children in lower Manhattan after the 9/11 attacks even more unbearable. All those flyers they passed out, juxtaposed with the footage of the planes impacting the towers, then the towers burning and the people in them at first waving for rescue and then abandoning hope and falling. Falling. Their skirts billowing, their suit jackets flapping. A few were holding hands. Falling. I hope the parents didn't look too closely at the news footage. I hope they didn't recognize a dress or a shirt or something, recognize their child falling, falling like tears down the face of a great structure stripped of its might. As I watched them fall I wanted to catch them. I don't think there's a flight attendant alive who saw that and didn't long to cup each one of those people in her hands and keep them safe. But all I could do was watch. I couldn't do a thing to save them and, Christ, I am so sorry for that.

I'S A SHAME I am going to hell, because I think heaven can use someone like me. Heaven can definitely do with a little lightening up, I say. But, according to the pallid people in long sleeves who handed out pamphlets on the beach where I grew up, hell is where I'm headed.

I swear, I was just following my mother. She'd position herself in front of me with her arm out like a traffic cop every time the religious-pamphlet people came toward us. "Stay back," she'd hiss, "this is *my daughter.*"

She announced that last part like it was some kind of universal call for propriety, and it worked. They stayed back, their pamphlets quivering in their pasty palms. But often they hollered at us as we passed: "You're both going straight to hell. Did you know that?"

I didn't think it was very fair that I should have to go to hell, too, but this was my *mother* here, and I couldn't go taking pamphlets from people she just finished hissing at. From the little I knew about hell, it sounded super uncomfortable. To avoid going there, I certainly would have accepted a pamphlet— even after the awful *Roe v. Wade* incident in Washington, D.C., the year before, when I accidentally accepted a pamphlet advocating legal abortions. My father snatched it out of my hand and slapped the shit out of me with it right there on the steps to the Lincoln Memorial.

I didn't think that was very fair, either. I did not even know what an abortion was, so of course I had to look it up when I got home. The only definition our dictionary offered was "of or pertaining to the act of stopping suddenly" or something like that. So I wondered why I got the crap slapped out of me because of a paper promoting the act of stopping suddenly, because what the hell is wrong with stopping suddenly? My own mother had done it in the car earlier that day. I practically still had a bruise from that braking-mom maneuver of hers in which she slung her arm out and slammed it against me in order to keep my unseatbelted ass from embedding itself into the dashboard. So I figured I learned a new word if nothing else, and then I got the crap kicked out of me all over again when my father found out I'd been telling people my mother had an abortion in the car.

Still nobody explained to me what was so bad about abortions. I had to find out for myself at the county fair, where an antiabortion group rented a booth and displayed a succession of plastic pink fetuses. They were arranged in ascending order according to age and size, and a fetus at four weeks looked like a pollywog to me, and I wondered why anyone would want one inside them.

My Life Sciences teacher had taught us about tapeworms the week before, and I wanted to know the difference between a fetus and a tapeworm. I mean, they both feed off you, don't they? And we kill tapeworms, don't we? In fact, that was the beginning of my tapeworm phobia, and I was pretty sure I even had a tapeworm living in me right then, as I always affected the symptoms of the disease of the week from my Life Sciences class. Earlier my teacher had taught us about arteriosclerosis and held up a big picture of a bisected clogged artery and told us the coroner could take this dead man's veins and snap them in half like raw spaghetti. After that I went a whole week without eating my customary truckload of Halloween candy for breakfast before someone finally informed me that candy doesn't contain a lot of cholesterol.

But tapeworms—now *that's* a whole different story. I was in the process of wondering if tapeworms were such bad things after all, since I was such a failure at being a bulimic. (I swear, you had to get up from the table right after you ate every single time in order to have a successful hurling. Otherwise, your stomach, which is your enemy, went on and digested everything.) I just couldn't muster the commitment it took, so it seemed to me a tapeworm was the ideal solution. All you had to do was sit there and let it leach up all your vitamins and minerals, and before you know it you're emaciated and on the cover of *Cosmopolitan*.

So I asked the man at the booth to explain the difference between a fetus and a tapeworm, and he told me people who have tapeworms go to the doctor, and people who have abortions go to hell. He was about to hand me a pamphlet when my mother jumped in and did the braking-mom maneuver right there, and we weren't even in a car. "Stay back," she hissed at the man, "this is *my daughter.*"

So of course I was really embarrassed, because there I was, having been put to a sudden stop, which means my mother just gave me an abortion right there in front of the antiabortion guy. And here I was hell-bound because of it. I felt really bad about it until my mother told me what she always told me when I was afraid of going to hell. "Jesus Christ, Hollis," she said, "what bigger hell is there than a heaven full of people like that?"

THE HEAD SURVIVED but the body didn't, and without a body it's hard to have a bobble-headed Chihuahua on your dashboard. Otherwise you've just got this plastic dog head on a spike, kinda, which normally you wouldn't think was such a tragedy, but it turns out I was really attached to the plastic Chihuahua.

"The head was supposed to go on the dashboard," I lamented to Daniel, "on top of a *body*."

I was gonna name the bobble-doll "Buford," and I was gonna be like an old person in a motor home driving around pointing at things, stopping at bowling-alley bars for a beer and stuff. It was a sweet dream now dead because I failed to bring the bobble-headed Chihuahua safely back from Tijuana, which is where I bought it. So here I am with only the head, and the torso is still in the belly of the plane somewhere, lurking in the shadows like a miniature murder victim.

God, I do not need to be thinking about this right now, because it brings to mind the notorious missing torsos of my neighborhood. I know I've been thinking about this a lot lately, the fact that the day before I closed on my house here in Capitol View the police found a severed human head in a sack on my street, but you have to admit the subject is pretty interesting. Especially when you factor in the detail that, strewn about, they later found six bags of other body parts all chopped up like Cobb salad. And here's the kicker, the bags of body parts *didn't match the bag of head parts*, and I don't think they ever uncovered the missing pieces to match the found pieces, let alone who the pieces once belonged to, or for that matter—and probably most important—who was responsible for separating the pieces from their main parts to begin with. So by my count there are at least two torsos still out there, headless and/or limbless, waiting to be stumbled over in the dark.

That's daunting, because stumbling in the dark is how I spend most of my life. Everything that's ever happened to me has been a misinterpretation of what I *meant* to happen. For example, I bought this house as an investment, figuring I'd turn it over after a year like the rightful nightmare most investors are to in-town communities. But instead I've lost work due to airline industry cutbacks, and I've had to reside here since, biding time. The house has more than doubled in value, something else I stumbled into, because if it were up to me alone, faced daily as I am with the drug addicts, whores, and crack dealers, I would have left this neighborhood long before that happened.

At least I am not alone anymore. My friends Honnie and Todd have moved into the neighborhood, and other creative-but-poor people who probably never smoked crack or sucked dick to get crack or killed anybody are moving here as well. It's a slow seepage, and it's nice and all, but Honnie and Todd in particular aren't faring well. They knew there was a crack house across the street when they moved in, but they didn't know there was a dealer living right next door. I also have a crack dealer living across the street from me, but the only bother he causes is the occasional traffic jam, seeing as how he provides a drive-by service. Honnie and Todd's drug-dealing neighbor, though, is very aggressive. He has already taken a baseball bat and smashed every single window in their house while they were out buying calk at Home Depot. There were plenty of witnesses, too, but all were too afraid to finger the guy to the police.

I go over there sometimes just to sit on their porch with them, so there will be a witness in case the drug dealer comes over with a bat again or something. But even if he did, the police would not be that helpful, not if their past lack of intervention is any indication. The gang fights and gunfights go on outside our doors all night. Occasionally I work an overnight flight and drive home in the early morning, which seems to be crack-whore happy hour in these parts, but at least there are fewer guns going off then. Three children have been killed in our neighborhood since I bought my house. Lary, who lives nearby, points out that one wasn't really a kid, but a big teenager who was killed by the police in the process of committing a crime, so he doesn't think that killing counts. I don't see why it shouldn't.

"Don't you see?" I ask. "He was just a kid."

He doesn't see. I can't believe he doesn't see. "What I see," he says, "is your mortgage, which is only four hundred and fifty dollars a month."

'M AMAZED THEY LET Lary on the plane. I always
am, not just because he looks like a curly-headed
crocodile—and all wide-eyed, too, like he's half a
second away from taking hostages—but because he
was flying standby using one of my airline-employee
buddy passes, and everybody knows traveling under those
circumstances is iffy at best.

He was flying to Cancun, Mexico, but only to pass
through on his way to Isla Mujeres, a tiny island off the
coast, where he expects to wallow in margaritas and the
saliva of young Mexican maidens. Grant was with him,
with much the same agenda, though Grant doesn't
much care from what gender the saliva is generated.
Grant cut off half his hair recently, which means
his hairdo has been reduced to the size of your
basic bushy shrub, as opposed to an entire tree, which always makes me think they're gonna make him purchase
an extra seat to accommodate his head mass, but the
agents let him on the plane, too, fantastically. Even so, it
doesn't amaze me as much that Grant made it on the
plane flying standby as the fact that there was Lary, sitting
right there on the aircraft, passengerlike, as if all his nutball molecules were not eminating a visible aura at all.

Gosh, I'm almost proud. I remember the first time
these freaks flew standby with me. We three plus Daniel
were on our way to Prague, because Daniel had picked it
out on a map of the world painted on the wall of a restaurant the week before, and we all had airline buddy passes
provided by me or friends of mine, which meant we were
just above deep-sea bottom feeders on the list of priority
to get on the plane. I'd warned them that they needed to
dress nice, as back then a jacket and tie were required for
airline nonrevenue travel, and I was not at all confident
they could pull it off. I know Daniel, for one, didn't even

own a tie, and the only suit jacket he had was made of blemished suede, which I myself had bought for a buck at a yard sale and had given him.

As for Lary, even though I was accustomed to his daily uniform of T-shirts stained with old egg yolks and whatnot, I'd remembered that the day I met him, which was outside a church minutes before his ex-girlfriend was about to marry another man, he'd been wearing what could pass for a presentable ensemble, with a tie that wasn't really a tie but one of those black leather twisty things knotted in the middle by an ornate clasp, which made it look like he'd barely escaped a lynching at the hands of evil fairies. So I knew Lary was capable of passing muster as far as dress is concerned, I just worried about that look he has. Seriously, from the neck up he looks exactly like Einstein's insane bastard son.

Grant was practically shaved bald back then, with none of the visible body piercings he has now, but until then all I'd ever seen him wear were faded overalls that were rolled at the cuffs and hung off him like loose hide on a diseased moose. It must have been a phase he went through, because today he is always downright dapper, even though it's not always a given he'll get on the plane when he flies standby on an airline buddy pass. Take the time when, even though he tried hard to keep the side of his head with all the metal impaled on it away from the gate agent, she spotted it anyway and wouldn't let him board until Grant talked her into letting an actual aircraft mechanic show up with a toolbox to unpierce him.

But that day years ago when we left for Prague, the three of them knocked on my door in the morning before our flight, and I opened it to find quite a presentable passel of gents, I must say. We left for the airport not knowing whether we'd make it, but knowing if we didn't we'd just choose a different route or destination, or both, it didn't matter. They stood by with me that day and they have ever since.

Really, like anyone, there have been hundreds of people who provided passing blips on the lifelong radar of my acquaintance, like sugar through a kitchen colander they were, but for some reason these three are among the lumps that stuck with me and always will. They are like boogers that can't quite be flicked free from the finger of my heart, because I have tried, believe me.

Over the years I have tried to run them off. Take the time I broke into Daniel's house and stole all his tequila, or the time I broke into Lary's house and stole all his hair products, or the time I broke into Grant's house and didn't steal anything, but I did rearrange all his furniture, which to him is worse. After that they hated me for exactly as long as it took for them to love me again, which was about five minutes. And vice versa. They're not angels, either, believe me. Take the fax campaign Lary waged on me in my home eight years ago, page after page of just two words: "You Cunt!" But I forgave him and he me and eventually I stopped asking why these three wouldn't leave like everyone else and simply started being thankful they were always there, standing by.

Get It Up

THIS PLACE IS SO nice I normally could not afford it even if I back-charged for all those gratuitous blowjobs I gave in college, but here I am all bundled under the down comforter even though the weather is really mild outside. I'm on a layover at the Hermitage Hotel in Nashville goddam Tennessee, and I have the *room service* menu in my hand, I swear. I'm gonna order something even though I'm secretly afraid that as I try to sneak out tomorrow I'll get pounced on by the cordial people in the reception area, who will remind me, cordially, that I can't leave until I fork over the five hundred dollars extra I owe for in-room chicken fingers complete with miniature bottles of individual catsup.

But when I checked in they did not ask me to hand over a credit card. They just gave me the goddam key! The handle is broken on my suitcase, and the bellhop carried it to my room cradled in his arms like a large child even though I kept telling him he could extend the other handle and just roll it along the floor. He declined politely, and then I realized those floors are part marble. My suitcase is as battered and jagged as a broken grocery cart, and it makes a shrill keening sound when you roll it. I've been deaf and blind to it lately, but nothing like interjecting your crap-ass suitcase in surroundings like this to trigger a miracle cure. I'd have been embarrassed if I was still the easily embarrassed type.

But thank God I'm not. I have skin as thick as nickels. At the airport our crew was met by a driver carrying a sign, and he was very officious until I actually—I am not kidding—*fell out* of the van and landed flat-ass in the gutter. At the time I was totally out of uniform, wearing Grant's tangerine swing coat, and damn if my heel didn't catch in the cuff. It sent me sailing out of that car like a flapping, wild-eyed albatross. I hit the ground like a sack of cement. People came running from across the street to make sure I was all right. "I swear," I laughed, "I'm fine."

Hell, that was *nothing*. I have fallen down before, and I've stayed down, too, pinned there underneath all my own demons. I laid there and let my brain become my enemy. For example, by the time I'd started interviewing with the airlines after college, I'd already been very enthusiastically laid off from my two previous jobs, my most recent boss having helped me along my way by literally tossing my personal office equipment out the door as I frantically called my mother from a pay phone across the street.

She herself had just lost her job due to government cutbacks, and had traded in her Buick for an old VW van that she was using to haul stuff to the swap meet, where she'd lay out a plastic tarp and set out her secondhand wares. When she came to get me that day, she had emptied the van of most of those wares, which included a box of broken ceramic beagles, to make room for my dinosaur desktop computer and other office tackle that had survived the tossing. She was half finished packing up my stuff when she noticed me still sitting there on the curb, crying.

"Get your ass up," she said to me, exasperated. "I said get it up."

Normally she would have taken me for pie at a local coffee shop afterward, but she was broke herself, owing in no small part to the fact that I had used her American Express card to pay my rent the month before. The past half year had been a hard (and, for my mother, expensive) period of perspective adjustment for me regarding my mother's transition from well-paid missile scientist to self-employed junk purveyor in partnership with her best friend Bill, and at that point it had almost, but not fully, settled in my head that I could no longer depend on her to supplement my meager-to-absent income as I pursued cool-sounding but low-paying pee-on positions at artsy magazines.

"What's this?" I asked when we'd finished, indicating a metal-looking apparatus on her dashboard. "That's my coin belt," she said proudly as she put the van in gear and we left the curb. "Isn't it neat?"

Coin belt? I thought, and at that I let go of my last toehold in denial regarding my mother's situation. It had come down to coins for her, literally, and how many she could collect.

"Yes, it's neat," I agreed, and burst forth with a whole new set of sobs. She kept asking me if I was all right, and I said I was. The next week I began looking for less-glamorous jobs with paychecks that could cover my bills. Until I found one I got up at 5 A.M. every weekend to help my mother set up her booth at the swap meet. It turned out there is little time for staying down when you've got boxes of broken ceramic beagles to sell.

"Are you all right?" the driver kept asking, all worried as he helped gather my fallen-ass self off the curb. "I really am," I assured him. I mean, seriously, what good am I if I can't get my ass up?

GRANT HAS ALWAYS WANTED a beehive hairdo, which is news to me. I mean, you think you know your friends and what they've always wanted, because always having wanted something is a pretty big part of your personality. But Grant had kept his beehive-hairdo desire kind of quiet until yesterday, when suddenly he ploughed through my front door talking about beehives like they've been on his mind since he was born.

"I cannot *wait*," he kept saying, pacing back and forth, his hands looking for something to squeeze. "I've got an appointment at the beauty parlor this afternoon!" he shrieked, pinching me in half with a bear hug.

Grant's hair, pre-beehive, reminds me of a big, thick ball of brown yarn being attacked by bats. It's all uncoiled and long and alive somehow. I can't imagine his hair structured into a stiffened upsweep, but Grant says that's exactly the reason he's been growing it out all these years. "I've always wanted a beehive hairdo," he said, adding that I should have known because he has a painting by Sister Louisa he sometimes displays in his living room. The subject is a librarian with a beehive, and the caption reads, "The Higher the Hair, the Closer to God."

"Girl, where have you *been*?" Grant chided me before setting off to the hair salon.

I heard they charged him double because he took up triple the time of a normal appointment, but damn, the result was fine. A full foot high, his beehive was a wonder in construction, and so stiff it could deflect a shower of sharpened axes. At the Local, where Grant bartends, hordes of people piled in to view the 'do, having heard about it, and Grant made a fortune in tips.

"I wonder if I can keep this thing for

Trashy Bartenders with Beehive Hairdos

another day," Grant laughed the morning after, but he'd already removed thirty-three hair pins, and worried simultaneously that he might have destroyed the hairdo's foundation and that the hairdo might just be indestructible after all, since after removing all that metal the beehive still stood there, unweakened, sturdy as ever, like it was frozen in Formica. "It's never going away," Grant said, awed.

Of course it's never going away. I know about trashy bartenders with beehive hairdos, as Grant is not the first beehived bartender I ever met. In grade school, I used to walk to the same bar every day after class, where I was practically babysat by a bartender named Kit. The bar, called the Tin Lizzy, was my father's hangout. It was located next to a liquor store owned by a man who I thought sure took a long time to tuck in his shirt whenever I went in there to buy penny candy. It turns out he was masturbating back there behind the counter, but that's another story.

Kit had a beehive bleached the color of cotton balls, and she actually kept things stored in there; pens, check stubs, dollar bills. Her hair was as thin as duck down, so these items clung there as if caught, like moths in a web, and you could even see the lines the leaded pencils left on her scalp.

Kit's shift started at 6 A.M. and my father would arrive every morning after breakfast and stay the day. His routine was so predictable that my sisters and I listed the Tin Lizzy as my father's daytime phone number on our school documents.

Kit knew my father, who had lost his job selling trailers again, was tipping her with my mother's money, so she let us eat all the potato chips and processed-beef logs we could stand, and kept a supply of quarters on hand so we could play pool, air hockey, and Pong until 5:30 when we'd walk home to meet our mother, who, surprisingly, held Kit in low regard.

"She's trashy," my mother would say, but didn't explain further.

Sometimes Kit would stay after her shift and let my father and other guys buy her beers, so I saw her drunk more than once, but drunk adults were nothing new to me. I even walked in on Kit in the bathroom once, sitting there on the toilet with her panties around her ankles. I screamed I was so mortified with myself, but she calmed me down and told me to come inside and close the door behind me.

"Listen, kid," she said, and I could see there were lots of stripes on her head from all the pencils she'd put there earlier, "don't hang out at bars anymore. Tell your dad to take you somewhere else. There's not even any windows here, for chrissakes."

I have to say I was surprised, because I thought Kit liked having me there every day, but here she was, literally, telling me to get out.

"Get out," she said, and damn if she didn't start bawling her eyes out right then. "Get out," she repeated, and I would have left right then but she had a hold of my hand, so I stayed with her until she let go. To this day I'm amazed at the resilience of that memory, the image of Kit crying on the toilet, clutching my hand, the incredible awkwardness of that moment. I'm trying to do what she said, I'm trying to get out, but to this day I still have a soft spot in my heart for trashy bartenders with beehive hairdos.

Do Crazy

NEVER ASK GRANT'S ADVICE, because usually he'll only tell you one of two things: "Suicide," or "You need to fuck a fat black man." Personally, I don't think either qualifies as real guidance, but I guess it depends on who you are.

Take Lary, for example, though I doubt he ever fucked a fat black man, I have to wonder about the suicide part.

As far as I know, Lary is still alive, but not for a preponderance of effort. Almost annually he ends up in the hospital because he flung himself off the top of something. He argues this is just a hazard of his job, which has to do with production lighting and involves a lot of scaffolding and ladders and whatnot, combined with the fact that he likes to take acid while climbing things. "I'm not suicidal," Lary says.

"Ha! You are a lying goddam sack of rabid bats!" I tell him. "What about the *gun*? You had a goddam *gun* to your head once!"

Here I'm just going by what he told me. I never actually saw Lary point a gun to his own head, though the mental visual I can conjure is very pleasing. No, the gun incident is what Lary himself told me he did way back when his neighborhood was even more of a crime-ridden shit pit than my own, and people often tried to break into the dilapidated warehouse Lary calls a home—or they simply knocked on his door, which Lary hates just as much.

So Lary bought a gun and waved it around with his drapes open, which was only half effective in keeping criminals away. So then he started wandering the street in front of his warehouse, waving the gun around and shouting, which was a little more effective. But the problem wasn't completely eradicated until he started wandering the street, shouting, waving the gun around, and then pointing it to his own head!

"After that nobody came near me," Lary says. "It was great."

"That's right. Do crazy," Grant concurs, finally adding a third piece of advice to his standard string. "It works every time. People stay away from crazy. People are *afraid* of crazy."

Grant learned this after he bought a run-down house in Kirkwood with a dead chicken nailed to the doorjamb and a drug club across the street where crack whores evidently went just to get roughed up. In the first three months they stole fifteen hundred dollars worth of landscaping equipment from Grant, as well as his entire illegal collection of taxidermied endangered animals.

At that point Grant thought the appropriate measure would be to get tough, so he stood vigil in his living room night after night, and the second he saw a miscreant set foot on his lawn he would sound the house alarm, an ear-piercing shrill he thought surely would train them, Pavlovian-style, not to come near his house.

He was wrong. They stole his ex-wife's entire collection of heirloom Christmas decorations next, as well as other stuff. "I'd always see people in the neighborhood wearing my clothes," he laughs. He sold that house the next year, then bought another one near me in Peoplestown.

At first people stole from him there, too, making for some well-dressed crack addicts in Peoplestown, but then Grant met Papa Smurf, a wizened, drug- and alcohol-addicted neighborhood fixture, whose habit was to stand on the sidewalk and stare at Grant through rheumy eyes every afternoon. When Papa Smurf finally approached Grant, he was wearing shoes too big and too familiar.

"Is you a saint?" he asked.

"No," Grant answered, "I am not."

Papa Smurf must not have believed him, because he took to confessing to Grant on a regular basis. "God has given me the affliction of addiction," he'd say, then he'd totter off to his apartment located above a corner market across the street, where he lived alone. Nobody ever bothered Papa Smurf.

So Grant asked his advice. "How do I keep people from bothering me?" he said. Papa Smurf considered Grant's question, and then offered this wisdom: "Don't do mean. Mean don't work," he counseled. "Do crazy. People's *afraid* o' crazy."

As it turns out, Grant does crazy very well. He festooned the outside of his house with crack lighters, painted religious figures and plywood signs with sayings like, *God is coming, repent immediately.* Nobody bothered him again. A few months later, Papa Smurf died alone in his apartment. He'd been dead four days before officials gained access to his home, where they found him near the door, on his knees.

"Four days in ninety-degree heat," says Grant, remembering that he'd watched from his porch as the coroner carried a shovel up the stairs to remove Papa Smurf's body.

After that Grant didn't care much about his stuff anymore. He gave it all away. Seriously. He invited people over to take what they wanted. I got a concrete Virgin Mary painted "haint" blue, a pair of wooden shoes, and a lamp stand covered in crack lighters. Lary took a mechanical nun that breathes fire. In the end, Grant started life over with little more than one pair of shorts and eight pairs of prescription sunglasses. Of course we all think he's insane, he wouldn't have it any other way. "Don't do mean. Do crazy," he says. "People's *afraid* o' crazy."

CAN'T BELIEVE I was conscious when my head was cracked open, and for the record I'd like to say I've always resented how my family blames me for it and refers to the incident as the time "Holly cracked her head open." It's not like I picked up the brick my own self and hit my head with it. The brick was thrown at me by an asshole neighborhood kid. He stood in the courtyard of our apartment building maybe six feet away with the brick in his hand, shouting, "Little girl, you better move because I'm gonna throw this brick."

My sister Cheryl was with him. "Move, Holly, he's gonna throw the brick."

A gaggle of neighborhood kids were there as well. "Move, because he's gonna throw that there brick."

Of course I didn't move, I was *two*, for God's sake. I didn't know what the hell they were talking about. Besides, only four days earlier I had taken my mother's cricket cage full of family jewelry and passed it out among these very same kids to ensure their undying friendship. Surely they wouldn't allow harm to happen to me after that, would they?

Those ungrateful, two-faced little shitholes. They let that boy throw the brick. To this day, I think back and I'm amazed, because it's not like the courtyard was small and narrow and my twenty-pound, two-year-old ass was taking up the entire sidewalk. Though I heard him, it still made perfect sense, even to my baby brain, that if the boy wanted to throw the brick, he could easily aim at an *empty* spot.

My father said my head qualifies as an empty spot, but he was happy I survived and joking was his way of showing it. Besides, my head was not empty, it was full of blood and stuff. Our babysitter, a big Hawaiian lady who slept in a hammock in her living room, kept saying, "So much blood in such a little body." She was in a good position to gauge, too, because she'd laid me on the couch in the living room and hung my head over the armrest so the blood could drip directly into a Pyrex mixing bowl. Cheryl kept bringing the kids by to see my brains, which I don't think were actually showing, but she kept pointing to the crack in my head anyway, saying, "Look, brains!" and they believed her.

The doctor stitched my brains back in my head and when my parents confronted the boy who threw the brick, he just shrugged and said, "I told her to move." In grade school I took to parting my hair directly down the center, which exposed the scar. If someone asked about it, my family would say, "That's where Holly cracked her head open," and I couldn't believe they still blamed me for that.

Later I fell in love with a boy three years ahead of me in high school. He had eyes like wide horizons, and my breath would quicken the second I saw his face. God, did I adore him, with my heart hung out there like a freshly caught fish, all exposed to the air and gasping.

This boy was an adventurist, though, and he was only sticking around, he said, until he'd earned enough money to move to Australia, where he planned to spend the rest of his life surfing and bussing tables at a seaside diner. Though I heard him I always figured things would work out anyway. Maybe he would take me with him or maybe he wouldn't go, after all.

He used to take me to the beach in San Clemente so we could surf next to the nuclear-power plant, where the waves were supposed to be really awesome. I never did catch on, though. Surfing has got to be the hardest sport known to man. To this day I don't understand the appeal of bobbing around in big waves with a bunch of wooden torpedoes darting at your skull. So I would sit on the beach and watch, and when he came in from the ocean I would cling to him like locks of his own hair.

He would always tell me about Australia, how the waves were bigger than buildings and people still lived off the land like pioneers. He had visions of himself sleeping in a mud hut off the highway, which ran along the beach, and in the mornings he would roll up his meager belongings, stash them behind a tree, and surf until it was time to clock in at the diner, where they wouldn't mind that he showed up for work soaking wet every day.

They were big dreams, but not big enough for me to fit in there anywhere. He dumped me after driving me home from one of those San Clemente excursions. I remember when he extricated himself from me, crying and stuck to him like I was. "How can you do this to me?" I blobbered. He shrugged and said, "I told you I was moving."

I'd heard him, too, but I figured he wouldn't throw the brick with me standing there. He did, though, and looking back I'm amazed at how many times in my life I let myself get hit in the head with that same brick. I wonder how many more times it will happen before I finally get out of the way.

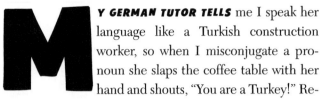

MY **GERMAN TUTOR TELLS** me I speak her language like a Turkish construction worker, so when I misconjugate a pronoun she slaps the coffee table with her hand and shouts, "You are a Turkey!" Regardless of her opinion, though, I'm still a foreign-language interpreter for the airline where I work. So on the plane I'm known as the "speaker" flight attendant. I don't mind because it makes me feel important and I get to boss people around.

For instance, just the other day, a man refused to properly stow his carry-on bag. You know, it's very important to make sure everything's in its place before we back away from the gate. It's not okay to put your boombox on your lap or your baby in the overhead bin. No. Everything has to be just right before we can announce to the captain that the cabin is secure and we can get going. That's the important part, isn't it? To *get going*.

But this flight wasn't going anywhere. We couldn't leave until this man seated in the back of the plane secured his carry-on luggage. Some of the other flight attendants thought he was acting suspiciously because he seemed so reluctant to surrender his baggage. So I was summoned. I was the "language interpreter" after all, and therefore automatically dispatched to deal with stuff like this.

Upon first glance I thought right away I'd have trouble communicating with this particular passenger. He might have been Middle Eastern, or maybe Italian, neither of which is a region where I know the language. His body was wedged in his coach-class seat like a big ball of softened cheese, and a spiky-haired mole the size of a sea urchin grew out of his ear. He was probably sixty, and his breath hung so heavily in the cabin you could actually *feel* it on you.

On his lap was a big black bag. I tried German. I tried Spanish. I tried English. Those were all the languages I knew and still I couldn't convey to him that he needed to give up his bag to be stowed before we could back away from the gate. But the passenger's German was even more indecipherable than my own, and the only English word he knew was "you." Somehow, though, I understood there was something inside the bag he needed with him right then, so through charades I convinced him he could take out the things he needed, and we could store the rest in the bin above him, and that way we could get going. So I watched him rifle through the bag's contents and retrieve one item: it was an eight-by-ten glossy black-and-white photograph.

He thrust the picture at me, smiling and shouting the only English word he knew. "You," he roared. "You, you, you."

I took the picture and looked at it. It showed a slim, handsome young man in a cavalier pose, looking up as if he were caught in the act of laughing at an off-color joke. It looked like a publicity still from the fifties, except his hair was a little too long and lustrous. Maybe he was a young king.

"You," the passenger said again, indicating the photograph. I told him I didn't understand what he wanted. He took the picture out of my hands, pointed to it and then to himself. "You, you, you," he said again, and then he laughed. For the first time I really looked at the passenger's face, his cauliflower-shaped face, and suddenly I understood. The picture was of himself when he was young. He had gotten his pronouns mixed up, and when he said "you" he thought he was referring to himself.

The man's eyes looked back at me and sparkled like dark stars through crinkled sockets. He pointed to the picture. He pointed to me. He pointed to himself.

"You," he said, his finger aiming proudly at his chest.

"Me," I corrected him softly.

Me, I thought to myself. Then I took his baggage and secured it properly.

KEIGER CAN'T DRIVE WITH me behind the wheel without losing a few years off his life, he says, and Grant and Lary agree, which really pisses me off. I am a perfectly fine driver. I mean, between the four of us, I am not the one who dropped the dishwasher in the middle of the freeway. I'm not naming names, mind you, or even admitting that anything actually happened, but I will tell you that the guilty party has a smile that belongs on a big voodoo doll and the dishwasher was mine.

Not that I ever saw it. I just got a call one morning from evil voodoo mouth man, who was at that moment perusing a bunch of expensive appliances from the fire sale of a failed dot.com enterprise. "Seriously, it's never even been used," he said of the dishwasher. "Not that you'd ever use it, either. I've seen your kitchen." That did it, of course.

"You retard, I would so use it, and not just to store bags of cat litter like you do in yours." I swear, I do not even know why Lary (oops, I said his name) *cares* about kitchen appliances. To hear him go on that day you'd think he cooks a turkey supper every Sunday, when in fact the only thing he has to eat in his house is half a bag of pistachios and half a dozen chocolate Easter eggs. It used to be a full bag and a full dozen, but goddam, a girl has got to eat when she's pretending to care for his cat while he's away, doesn't she?

So here Lary was getting me all excited about a new dishwasher when I already had one that worked perfectly fine. It was scarred and leaked a little bit, but it did it's job and I was fine with that. It just wasn't shiny and plated in nickel or whatever the new one promised. In fact, it was so beat up from the former owner of the house that I fig-ured he must have had parties in which he invited homeless people to come over and hit it with their shopping carts. There were pieces missing from it, too, like the silverware basket, which I'd replaced with a plastic salad strainer that worked fine. It wasn't all that quiet when it ran, either; in fact the sound was so loud that houseguests had once mistaken it for a helicopter SWAT team. Also, each cycle seemed to take twenty years and all the glasses came out afterward coated in some kind of calcified film. All the same, though, I would never have thought to replace it if Lary hadn't called and got me all convinced that a new dishwasher would change my life. "All right," I told him. "Get it for me and I'll pay you back."

Two entire days went by before I called him to politely inquire as to its whereabouts. "Where the hell is my goddamn dishwasher, you booger-eating loser?" I shrieked at him. I'd just spent the last forty-eight hours entertaining dishwasher fantasies in which I wore pedal-pushers, served appetizers from a tray, and accepted everyone's compliments on how sparkly all my barware was. Plus, I'd just seen a commercial for that same brand dishwasher that demonstrated its abilities, the best being that it could disintegrate an entire three-layer birthday cake with one cycle.

"I lost it," he said, and he sounded *serious.* I mean, normally he'd have any number of bizarre reasons at the ready for flaking on me. For instance, he once forgot to feed my dog and told me it was because he was forced to copulate with aliens to save the world. It just wasn't like Lary to not put any effort into lying to me. "Really, where is it?" I asked.

"Really, I lost it," he kept telling me. "It fell off the back of my truck."

"No, really."

"Really."

"No, seriously."

"Seriously."

There was a full fifteen minutes of this before I finally believed him, at which point, of course, I had to detonate. "What the *hell* do you mean *it fell off your truck?* What kind of extra-chromosome bottom-feeding fool loses a dishwasher?" I ranted, the whole while slowly coming to grips with the fact that I was now stuck with my original dented-ass dishwasher that sounds like a leaf blower and doesn't disintegrate birthday cakes, and somehow that just made my life a lot less enjoyable all of a sudden.

Here I was, starting to envision something new and different that offers all kinds of added excitement to my life, and then it gets pulled out from under me like a bad parlor trick, and suddenly my otherwise perfectly fine life up to then seems like a total turd pellet. It took me awhile, as I put my grit-covered glasses away in the cupboard, to re-appreciate my rusty wreck dishwasher with all its improvised parts. In the end the thing still works perfectly fine. Everything does. As with anything, pieces will always break and be replaced. None of us ever leave here whole, or not outwardly anyway. Everywhere you look are the patched up and put together, not new, but not uninteresting nonetheless. In the end, the very last thing it does is make life less enjoyable, and I am perfectly fine with that.

BILL WAS NOT at all very sympathetic about my tapeworm. He was too busy bitching about how prostitution was the only way to make money in Costa Rica. Seeing as how he was five hundred years old with bad eyes and *gout* (whatever that is), I had to tell him straight out that I doubted he could get much for his body, especially since there were so many pretty whores in Quepos for him to compete with, and most of them hanging out right there at his *pensione* bar.

He rolled his big, bad eyes and wondered again how I could be my mother's daughter. When he met my mother, he was living in his car. They met at a dusty auction house in Chula Vista, California, where they'd haggled over a box of mostly broken stuff. In the end my mother out-bid him.

"Good fight," he said, his cigarette hanging loosely from his lips like a little snapped appendage. "I'll buy half off you, whaddaya say?" My mother refused his offer, but they became best friends nonetheless. He was a decade younger, tall, big-eyed, and always about to burst into knee-slapping laughter. I personally think my mother had a crush on him. The fact that he lived in his car would have been in keeping with her tastes, I believe. She was not all that picky about people she had crushes on.

Bill had always insisted he was my stepfather, and I would not have put it past him to marry my mother on a platonic basis for whatever benefit they'd both receive, but my mother never mentioned it. They began selling the junk they'd acquired at these run-down auction houses at the local swap meet on Sports Arena Boulevard in San Diego. My mother had just been laid off from her job as a weapons de-signer and, rather than rally and find another position in the same industry like she normally did, she went into business with Bill instead.

As my mother's best friend, alleged second husband, and professed stepfather to me, he'd accepted the yoke of parental badgering from her at her passing. "You kids are like little liposuction tubes, you just *suck*. You suck everything out of everything. Suck, suck, *suck*. If your mother saw you now she'd die all over again."

At that time I was sucking on my second margarita. We drink a lot when we're around Bill, my sister and I, and to be around him these days we usually have to go through some South American jungle. Cheryl is his favorite, and she would be my favorite, too, if I were Bill. He likes people who don't hide their flaws, people who couldn't even if they wanted to. Cheryl is a former chain-smoking cocktail waitress living in Las Vegas, and I remember when she heard the news that her new uniform would include fishnets and a G-string.

"I'm gonna stuff my big, beautiful, size-12 ass in that G-string, whaddaya think about that?" she laughed. I've tried to visit her at work to see her in uniform, but that hotel is so huge I'd have better odds at running into old college chums at the airport, plus I heard the MGM has since included a cute peplum skirt as an option in the uniform, and the G-string is no longer mandatory.

So it was Cheryl who insisted I go see Bill, because "he's about ready to die, I swear, Holly. He probably has less than a year to live. He's got that gout, and it's really acting up."

"What the hell is gout?"

"I don't know," she said, exasperated, "he just has it."

So I went to Costa Rica to go see him, which was a huge gesture on my part because I hate that place. Already I'd been bitten by a dog, cut by rusty things, and *hit by a car*. I was just walking along the side of the road and a car pulled up and the next thing I knew I was rolling around on its hood, which is really embarrassing. I should have just gone home, but instead I took a bus to see Bill and sleep in his garage, which, until the week before, had been flooded. It cost ten dollars a night for a nice room in Quepos, but Bill had dried out his garage for me, and who can argue with hospitality like that?

"I think I breathed in a bunch of tapeworm eggs while I slept last night," I said. The mold smell in Bill's garage was so thick I'm probably still, to this day, growing mushrooms in my lungs.

"Suck, suck, *suck*," said Bill as he poured me another shot. He didn't look near dead to me. His eyes might have been big and bad, but they were the clearest blue eyes you ever saw, and he still smoked like a living chimney without coughing up organs or anything. I, on the other hand, was stiff and sore and wrapped in dirty Band-Aids like a decrepit mummy. God! I wailed inwardly, hanging my head. Why am I here?

I was there because Bill had proven to be a good friend to my mother, and therefore he was family to me. When she got sick he held her hand, fetched her prescriptions, and bitched about how the medical industry conspired to keep the cure to cancer under wraps so doctors could make more money. Bill doesn't die, his practice is to build new life. That's what he always does. Damn if he didn't up and make his fifth fortune after my mother died, and with that he opened that bar in Costa Rica. Now he's sitting here heartsick, with tourism practically at a halt, complaining that every cent is quickly getting sucked out of his life.

I half thought I could talk him into coming home with me, because if Bill did end up dying, I didn't want him to die in the jungle, but having been there and having seen him I know he will not die for awhile. "Stop complaining, you codger," I cough. "You're gonna outlive me, especially now that I have this tapeworm."

Bill beamed like a proud parent and then embraced me warmly. "A tapeworm," he sighed, "maybe you'll drop some of this weight."

JESUS GOD, I do not have a tapeworm after all. What I have, according to the majority of these eleven drugstore pregnancy tests, is a much more permanent problem. I keep going back to the store to buy more tests because sometimes the pink line isn't all that dark, and I think it might need to be darker for it to be real. On one there was no pink line at all, but that was just the one. On the other ten there were definitely pink lines in varying degrees of darkness, and ten-to-one are odds you just can't ignore.

A week later the doctor confirmed the drugstore diagnosis, so ain't life full of surprises.

Like it was just last Sunday we noticed that the Local finally put tables on their patio, and what a refreshing change it was to spend a sunny afternoon on a restaurant terrace drinking margaritas and watching the crack whores and homeless shuffle by rather than sitting at the requisite Virginia Highland coffeehouse watching the parade of soccer moms pushing jog strollers. We did see one mom at the Local, though. She was tattooed and tiny, and we wondered how she pushed out that infant without having to cut herself in half. The first thing she did after sitting down was take the milk bucket out of her bra and feed the baby.

"You see?" I said, "That's why I'd make a bad mother."

"Why?" asked Grant.

"I'm afraid I'd forget to feed it or something, and I'd come home one day and it would be dead on a bed of shredded newspaper like a neglected hamster."

Grant was speechless. Another surprise. "Girl," he repeated, "you got issues."

He's right. For example, rather than ac-cept the possibility that I had no biologi-cal clock, I worried my clock was just not ticking loud enough for me to hear and the day would come in the future when the alarm would go off and I'd turn into some kind of maternal sperm junkie, suddenly desperate, wearing my uterus on my sleeve, hoping someone would inseminate me before cobwebs covered my ovaries.

Which brings me to the whole childbirth bloodbath itself. Jesus, when my niece was born you'd have thought my sister was giving birth to a full-grown grizzly bear! I never saw so much blood and gore and . . . *growling*. I know I personally couldn't go through that without an IV bag of drugs as big as the baby itself. In fact, I'd like to start the epidural retroactively from the date of conception.

If I can just figure out when that was. Seriously, I'm so paranoid I can hardly have sex without wearing an entire scuba suit. So my theory is this: one night my uterus had an out-of-body experience while I was sleeping and latched itself onto the nearest man, who was probably right there in my bed, like a big fertile squid. That's the only way I can explain it, other than all that acrobatic sex—but the *armor*, I tell you, was in place! It's just that there must have been this minuscule, tiny, *microscopic* hole big enough for my entire future to fit through, that's all.

Lary did not shoot me, as he always benevolently offers to do when he sees me suffering. What he did, along with Grant and Daniel, was excitedly volunteer to be my bodyguard through the pro-life gauntlet on the way to the abortion clinic. "I could bring a pitcher of martinis," offered Grant. "It would be like a tailgate party!"

"Goddammit," I shrieked. I can't believe these three are planning my abortion like a trip to the beach. And Grant's martinis suck, by the way. He's on his Body Ecology diet again and he adds unsweetened cranberry juice to the vodka and his martinis always end up tasting like tart smegma. Not only that, since when was it just *assumed* I'd flush the sprogette?

"What am I, so fucking selfish that I can't fit this kid in my life?" I laughed, acting all brave, but really I was so scared that later I just sat in my room shaking, I mean *shaking*, like a drug addict overdue for a fix.

After my first obstetrics appointment I paid my toll to the parking attendant, who rose the restraining arm to allow my car through, but instead of driving away I simply laid my forehead on my steering wheel and sobbed so hard it felt like major organs were leaking out of my eye sockets. The attendant let me stay there until I finished, then handed me a tissue volunteered from a woman in one of the four cars waiting patiently behind me. "Everything will be all right," she said, not knowing what was wrong to begin with. "I know," I said, and thanked her. I drove away marveling at how I could hold up four cars and not one of them honked. Wow, I thought, life really is full of surprises.

'VE BEEN TOLD by trained professionals that my house is about to be sucked into the butthole to hell. Pretty much.

"See that right there?" one of them said, indicating a darkened border along the base of my foundation. "That there is moisture."

Evidently moisture is like flesh-eating bacteria to a house, and whenever it rains on my house, which it has done a lot lately, the water just sorta pools around its foundation, potentially rotting it right out from under me, causing the whole structure, over time, to kind of cave in on itself and ultimately disappear like that place in the movie *Poltergeist*, I'm guessing, but minus the maggots.

Instead there's mold. I wouldn't even have noticed it if one of the professionals hadn't shined a flashlight on it and pointed it out. "It's not even *fuzzy* yet," I told him. He looked at me like a neurologist might if he'd shown me an X-ray of my own personal brain tumor and I'd said, "That little thing? What's the big deal?"

In short, it's a big deal. Mold grows, and left on its own under a house it can thrive faster than a class-action lawsuit, releasing *spores* and things, which you *inhale*. So discovering even the tiniest little molecular bit of this stuff clinging to the foundation under your house is cause for panic, like finding anthrax in an air-conditioning vent.

So I had to call in the A-team, which for me is my contractor friend Art and his one employee, a bald, muscular, coffee-loving Lithuanian named Lucas. I hate to bother them because they are usually so busy building mansions and whatnot, and I always feel like my fix-it chores are so petty in comparison, like asking Michelangelo to paint the porch, but I don't want the UPS guy looking through my window and calling 911 because I'm on the floor with foam spilling from my nostrils that is much too green to be boogers.

"Well, since you put it that way," Art said, and he came right over. He brushed aside all the zillion-dollar estimates from the local foundation-repair mafia and said, "All these problems amount to one thing: You need to manage your flow."

So he and Lucas set about building a network of gutters and drains that allowed the rain to flow away from my house, rather than settle in my basement like a teeming pool of poison. God, this is *great*! I thought. I'm not absorbing the problem, I'm *deflecting* it.

It's the same philosophy they taught me in a self-defense class I took years ago: if someone is coming at you with a weapon, don't just crouch there and stave yourself to absorb the blow, *deflect* the damn thing. So when the instructor came at me with his rubber knife and pretended to attempt to stab me—moving with the speed of a deep-sea diver—I, without fail, deflected the blade right into his thigh muscle. I was just as good with the rubber gun, too.

"All you need to worry about is this little hole right here," the instructor said, pointing to the tip of the fake gun's barrel. "Just make sure it isn't pointed at you and you'll be fine." Then we'd spend the next fifteen minutes practicing the maneuvers we were taught, which amounted to deflecting the assailant's gun-holding hand to ensure the little hole wasn't pointed at our vital parts, so that if the assailant pulled the trigger before we could wrest the weapon from him, the bullet would hit one of our irrelevant parts, or, better, a bystander. "Manage the flow," our instructor told us.

"I *love* this," I told Grant while talking on my cell phone in my car. "That's how I'm gonna live my life from now on. I'm just gonna stay put and deflect stuff. I'm not gonna absorb anything. I'm just gonna manage the flow."

Grant is an expert at flow management. He once gave a party where he served only bread and wine, but had it all strategically situated in attractive settings throughout his art-laden house to instigate a flow pattern among guests that was conducive to lively conversation. ("Have you tried the multigrain? It's over there by the chair covered in crack lighters.")

"I know flow," Grant said, or at least that's what I think he said, because just then a Honda pulled in front of me and I had to brake so hard I could smell the rubber worn off my tires from the friction. The other driver stopped, too, but he hardly looked sorry at all. In fact, he almost looked like he thought it was *my* fault.

"That fucking prick, who the goddam fuck does he think he is? He's lucky I didn't crash into his ass and sue the shit out of him and the shit-eating idiots who insure him, can you fucking believe that? I cannot goddam *fucking* believe that cock-wagging asshole did not even *apologize*! Jesus goddam fucking *Christ*!" I hollered, the profanities flowing from me like water from a firehose, spewing and fuming until . . . what the hell was *that* now? What the goddam hell was that sound in my ear?

It took me a few moments before I realized it was coming through my cell phone head set. It was Grant, laughing. "Bitch," he said, "you don't deflect. You absorb. You are a *sponge*."

THE FORTUNE COOKIE SAID, "You will die cold and alone," and I'm glad I'm not the one who opened it. In fact, by the time it's opened Lary will be long gone, which kind of sucks all the fun out of stuffing false fortunes into cookies at Chinese restaurants, if you ask me.

"Don't you want to see their reaction?" I asked.

"Nah," Lary said. "I can envision it."

I figure if you're just going to *envision* the result of an elaborate prank, then you might as well envision the whole thing from start to finish. It's a lot easier than actually going to the restaurant, perusing their bowl of fortune cookies to pick out the ones whose real fortunes can be plucked from inside without disturbing their exterior, meticulously sliding the false fortunes inside, then covertly returning the tainted cookies back to the hostess stand.

"At the very least," I said, "you should keep the cookies and give them to your friends. You could make them open them right there."

"You want one?"

"Not the one that says I'll die cold and alone."

"You don't get to pick your fortune," Lary chided.

Christ, look who's talking, the big Fortune Fucker Upper, swapping real fortunes for fake ones, messing with the order in the universe, laughing in the face of Satan or any other fill-in-the-blank karma-related crap we get fed from birth. My own fate changed completely when I met Lary, who, at the time, was attending the wedding of his exgirlfriend Mary Jane, a wonderful girl he was a fool to let slip away. At the time I was on my way to being a normal person whose lot in life was to sit around burdened by a big sack of broken dreams like everybody else. But such are the dubious comforts of false fortune.

Lary spent many an hour with me barside at the original Vortex, talking me out of trying to fit in. He is nothing if not benevolent, you have to give him that. For example, he realizes that if he doesn't let the women in his life slip away they'll have him as the prize for their efforts, and he figures, rightly, that they deserve better. Besides, they don't slip very far. To this day Lary remains devoted to Mary Jane and her family. But that doesn't mean he won't die cold and alone, in fact I think he's determined to. I think that might be why he created all those false fortunes—so he won't be alone in dying cold and alone.

But right now Lary is cold but not alone, hence he's in the process of alienating all his friends to fix that. He won't answer our calls and still won't forgive me for giving up alcohol. If I called him right now he'd look at the display on his cell phone and ignore it. Sometimes I call him using Grant's phone, because Grant is one of the few people whose phone calls Lary will take, not that that's a good thing, because Grant is trying to talk Lary into moving to Mexico to live on a boat.

"Jesus God!" I bitched at Lary over Grant's phone. "Don't buy a boat. You'd be buried in barnacles the first month!"

But even as I said that I realized Lary *is* a barnacle. He's got that crusty exterior, with hair the color of hay; he's a salty dog that somehow ended up living in a dilapidated warehouse in Atlanta. He bought the place for nothing a decade ago, now it's worth a fortune that's all his if he sold it, which he easily could. He's talking about moving to Isla Mujeres, an island in the Caribbean off the coast of Mexico. In fact, Isla Mujeres is where Grant once retired, having promised never to return to the dregs of normal society. That retirement lasted about five minutes before he was back ass-deep in the dregs, but Grant returns to the island every chance he gets, and the way he talks about the place makes us all long to go.

So that's where I am right now. I've my own shit to sift through, obviously, and I wanted desperately to be alone to do it. Grant recommended a $35-a-night hotel, "with cold cold air-conditioning in the room and hot hot water in the shower," which, now that I'm here, makes me wonder what he was comparing it to. I mean, the air conditioning is cold, sure, if you compared it to the breath of a dying person, and the shower water is hot if you compared it to refrigerated urine samples. "So fuck you," I e-mail Grant, but I can almost hear him laughing. He knows it's just the dregs talking, having clung to me from home, and he knows they will drop away soon enough.

And they did. I feel better now, and not in small part because I'm surrounded by such simple beauty. I spent yesterday alone but not cold, lying at a languid angle to the remarkably calm ocean, the horizon a parfait of blue hues, the air warming me like a womb. Suddenly a sense of gratitude washed over me like the ocean itself. I was thinking about my fortunes. There are so many, false and otherwise. From now on I'll be better, I promise, at distinguishing the two.

KNOCKED UP AS I AM, I'm afforded what is for me a rare view, which is that of being the only sober person at the party. But that's life. At first, when I realized this would be my lot in life for, like, pretty much *ever* (I mean let's face it, I can't be a boozer with a baby on my hip, how unattractive is that?), I thought, "Jesus God, what's left to live for?" I mean sure, there's *food*, but that was only fun for the first three months, when I got to pretend the whole world was my personal trough. You should have seen my car; it was a rolling wasteland of crumpled fast-food packets from drive-through joints, the floorboards crusted with dried cola. So that period was neat while it lasted, but when my body reached walrus status, my appetite kicked out of overdrive and I woke up one day full for good, so now the glut fest is finished and I'm back to wondering why I should get out of bed in the morning.

Then I felt my baby's first kick and it all came together. . . .

Yeah, right! Fooled you. The fact is I haven't reached that special moment of repose just yet. You know, *the moment*, that special revelation in which momhood and other cosmic thresholds suddenly come together in one big Birkenstock earth/heaven harmony. If this revelation is real I hope it comes soon, because as it stands I'm still freaked about the fact that this thing I'm growing inside me has eyeballs (I mean, you know, hopefully) and is going to be, like, *looking* at me soon, if not already. I wonder if it can see my kidneys.

And I wonder why I keep thinking of my mother's friend, Bitsy, a lovable fossil from Hollywood's heydey who used to be Burgess Meredith's personal clerk and who claims to, back in the fifties when she was a crimson-lipped bombshell, have had sex with both Gene Kelly and Fred Astaire, but not at the same time. When my mother met Bitsy (at work, where she designed weapons for the American government and Bitsy was her secretary), Bitsy's glory days were long gone but she still boasted a head of hair like Lucille Ball. They became fast friends that first day, when, sensing my mother's cigarette withdrawal, Bitsy tossed her a Salem and said, "What are you, a fuckin' nun?" That was in Santa Monica in the mid-seventies.

In San Diego almost two decades later, my mother didn't crave companionship like you would have expected of a dying person, but Bitsy was fiercely devoted to her nonetheless and tried constantly to contact her. "Tell Bitsy Mom can't come to the phone," I was instructed to shout from her bedside, and my brother would tell Bitsy my mother couldn't come to the phone. "Have her call me when she feels better," Bitsy pleaded in her craggy, tobacco-shredded voice.

But my mother never felt better. She died, as it so happens, in my arms. Bill was there, too, holding her hand. It's not as romantic as it sounds. At the time I was helping her sit upright in bed because her breathing had become labored, and I didn't expect her to die right then, but she did. Her last words, spoken about fifteen minutes earlier, were used to request a cigarette. There was no moment of repose in which she became serenely reconciled with her inescapable fate and gathered us about her bed to bestow words of wisdom. I remember nothing like that. I remember her fighting with the ferocity of a rottweiler to hang on to every last second of her life, even if it meant unimaginable pain and self-inflicted solitude to protect her good friend from her suffering. *That's life*, and this woman didn't want to lose any of it. Today, when I feel my baby kick—and I do, I wasn't making that part up—that's what I think: *that's life*.

Back in my mother's bedroom that day, after her breathing stopped, I gently placed her back on her pillow, and just then the phone rang. My brother peeked his head through the door. "It's Bitsy," he whispered.

Silence. "Tell Bitsy Mom can't come to the phone," I said.

GRANT IS LOOKING for Jesus on eBay, which is new. Normally he looks for Jesus in dumpsters, or under musty piles of old clothes at junk stores. Once he found a fabulous Jesus at a parking-lot flea market just south of Soddy Daisy, with the forehead all bleeding from the pointy brambles and everything. Sometimes Grant doesn't have to look at all. Sometimes people see all kinds of Jesus and call Grant to tell him where to go. Sometimes they even call *me* and tell *me* to tell Grant where to go. "I saw some great Jesus at the new Dollar Store on Moreland," a recent phone message said. "Don't forget to tell Grant."

This must mean Sister Louisa is back in full force. She must have come here in her 1974 copper-colored Ford Pinto and set up camp in Grant's head again, because Lord knows there is room. Yes, she is back now, in a big way, beehive and all.

"I found a *huge* paint-by-numbers of Jesus riding a donkey through Jerusalem," Grant exclaims, but I keep looking at his head, because I can't believe his hair doesn't have a residue of some kind, like a film of space-age polymer left over from his latest beehive. I swear Grant's hair is like a storm cloud, a roiling mass of curly hay that shoots out of his head like fibrous lightning. It takes two beauticians armed with eight cans of industrial lacquer to tame it into a mile-high hairball, and it's a serious wonder the result isn't permanent, but the whole thing really does just wash out at the end of the day.

"Bitch, did you not hear me say I found me a Jesus on a *donkey*?" he repeats, and I admit I'm impressed. My favorite Sister Louisa piece of all time depicted that very scene, with the donkey saying, "Who is this Jesus and why is he on my back?" It was sold years ago, back when Sister Louisa first started making her assemblages while living in the Airstream trailer of Grant's imagination. It was a doublewide trailer. Did I not say there is a lot of room in Grant's head?

I personally found my first Jesus in a thrift store in Costa Mesa when I was six. This Jesus had an imploring expression on his face and held out his hand like he was trying to coax a gun away from someone who just threatened suicide. I remember thinking, Who is this Jesus and what does he want me to put in his hand?

I found Jesus again in college, when an extremely horny follower of his named Jerry introduced us. Jesus and Jerry were buddies, I guess, because Jerry gave me his personal Bible and helped save my soul by convincing me to ask Jesus into my heart and shit—right there on my damn knees with Jerry's sweaty palm on my head and his khaki-clad boner not half a foot from my face. Then Jesus went and told Jerry I wouldn't "best represent" him as a wife, and Jerry dumped my barely saved self. He said he had to go where Jesus guided him. As I gave Jerry back his Bible, as he left me there, literally, on the side of the road, I remember thinking, Who is this Jesus and why is he guiding people down my pants?

Then Sister Louisa was born. Grant and Daniel and I had gone out in Grant's truck to sift through garbage in the back streets of Tuscaloosa, and in the dusk we came upon an abandoned trailer, its back end crumpled like a discarded beer can. That night, as the sun buried itself burnt orange in the background, Grant stuck his hand through the window of that trailer to grab some old pots off a stovetop, and that is when we heard the voice.

"Who the hell there?" it boomed from inside the trailer. "I say-yed, who THE HELL there?"

Grant's eyes popped out of his face like canned snakes, then he jumped behind the wheel of his truck and we peeled out of there like TV hooligans in a seventies crime drama.

Daniel and I were laughing so hard we thought we'd cough up

our own shoes, because we'd just seen the great Grant Henry get caught burglarizing a homeless man living in an abandoned trailer. "Wanna check to see if there's any pencils we can steal from blind beggars?" I teased him, but Grant was not listening to me. He had stopped all of a sudden, in a little mill village dotted with ramshackle shotgun shacks, and he was staring transfixed at a vision from his front window.

"Look at her," he kept saying. "Just look at her." I followed his gaze, which rested on a tiny, ancient woman sleeping in a chair on the other side of a screen door, her dark skin withered like pressed autumn leaves, her body comfortably sunk into itself like a stack of warming dough. Her hands were folded in her lap like two tiny pet cats. We sat silently looking at the lovely little mummy for a few moments as the weak light from her shack illuminated her silhouette. "She is Jesus," Grant gasped, and we all agreed. This is exactly how Grant Henry found Sister Louisa, sitting there sleeping on the side of the road.

I **CAN'T BELIEVE** how picky men are about penises. You'd think they were women. And women, I swear, really aren't that picky. As long as it functions we figure it's a perfectly good penis, whether it's the size of a totem pole or not, and if a girl tells you any different she's pulling that fake-chaste, I've-only-been-with-one-other-man-and-that-was-against-my-will crap that we all master in order to make you feel great about your own pocket-packin' status, which, *I swear to God,* is fine. We love it. Really. Whether it looks like it's been carved out of marble or not. Which brings me to my real point: circumcision, and the lack thereof.

You might wonder what business circumcision is of mine, since some people have argued that I have no penis of my own. But knocked up like I am, and freshly informed that the linebacker in my belly is, in fact, a boy, I say I'm gaining ground. On the sonogram last month—and we got a fuzzy view when the baby interrupted his break dance to bend over and moon us from behind—I saw it there plainly onscreen, kinda, in all it's tiny, adorable glory: my penis.

Until now I never knew I wanted one. But now that I have one I'm very protective of it, and it seems to me that the last thing any self-respecting penis-possessing person would want is to have someone come near their crotch with a scalpel, even if that person is wearing a surgical mask with a tank of anesthetic strapped to his back. I mean, please, *stitches* are involved, and a human-error factor, *down there*. I thought I would get some support on this stance from a few of my fellow tripods—I mean, they were *born* with their penises—but surprisingly I've been abandoned by my guy camp on this.

I voiced my hesitation to my genetic counselor, putting it this way, "Can you give me a good, sound, medical reason to perform circumcision—which is *surgery*, right?—on my son?" To which she answered, simply, "No." But they didn't think a person sitting behind an actual desk in an actual office inside an actual hospital was qualified as an authority on the "snip" debate, so instead they turned to their own pathetic company to back themselves up.

In classic gang-up mode, they first tried the archaic hygiene defense, and I don't want to go into detail, but the word "cheese" was bandied about. But please, maybe back before we had showers and soap and *loofahs*, and people routinely washed off in pig troughs, and men wore boxers made out of tobacco leaves, maybe then the hygiene argument had some merit. So hygiene explains why the pruning practice got started, but not why we kept it up.

I was especially surprised that Lary pounded the pro-snip line. Lary, who, even though he lives in an alleyway, still has a shower bigger than my kitchen, and has collected enough soap and oils and conditioner and scented enemas and stuff that his whole body could be covered by a big foreskin and he'd still be the cleanest, best-smelling man I know. And he's not even gay.

In all, their argument for circumcision amounts to the need for better washcloth access. This is a reason for surgery? God! Why not cut the lips off your face for better toothbrush access? Because, sure, it would work, but what's wrong with leaving your lips where they are and just parting them when it's time to scrub the hidden bits, if you know what I mean? So sorry, I don't buy the Big Snip ritual just to save my son a nanosecond in the shower every day, which brought the Clip Club down to their last defense: conformity.

"The other boys will make fun of him in the locker room," said Giant Michael, who, I would like to point out, has shirked conformity his entire life and become a successful restaurant owner and all-around cool hep cat because of it. But Michael was tired of me, and tired of defending circumcision, and made the mistake of trying to end the discussion by pointing out I sure had a lot to say for someone with no penis. But he was wrong, and this time I had the sonogram printout to prove it.

EVEN BEFORE SHE got shot at, I told my neighbor Honnie that if a bullet ever came through my window I'd be out of this place faster than my feet could carry me, and even then I'd assumed the bullet would have been by accident, that someone would have shot at someone else and my window just got in the way.

"I swear," I said to Honnie, "I'd be gone. You'd see my legs spinning underneath me like a cartoon character."

I don't remember what Honnie said next, but I wish I did, because in the end the bullet didn't go through my window, it went through hers. And it was no accident. Someone stood on the sidewalk in front of her house, aimed a gun at her living room and pulled the trigger. Three times. The bullets ripped through the curtains and chipped the tile on one of the fireplaces inside the home Honnie shares with her husband, Todd, and her mother, Bren.

"They didn't make much noise when they came through," Bren said sweetly of the bullets. "You'd think it would be louder than that."

If you want loud, you should have heard the girl who threatened Bren's life earlier that day. The police didn't think the incident merited the filing of a formal complaint, even though, when they arrived at the scene, the girl was still standing there screaming at Bren in front of her house. She was a little thing, the screaming girl, but God what a volcanic bitch she could be. According to her shrieks, Honnie's house was going to be blown up or burned down or both. The girl didn't even live in the crack house that started all this ruckus, the crack house in Capitol View that Honnie and her family were helping to close down. But the girl's boyfriend lived there so she felt it was her mission to go door-to-door on a campaign to convince people Honnie and her family were part of the Klan.

"Yeah, right," says Honnie as Snoop Dogg's "Ain't No Fun (If the Homies Can't Have None)" blares from the drug dealer's house next door (. . . *With a fat dick for your motherfuckin' mouth!*).

"This is the first place a white supremacist would want to live," she finishes wryly.

Honnie and her family aren't Klan members, they're artists, and they bought a house eight blocks away from me for the same reason I bought mine in Capitol View not long ago, because this neighborhood is the last bastion of affordable homes so close to the city. You can buy a house here with a mortgage for less than what you'd pay for a facial package at a day spa. They got a good house, too, better than mine, even. It has four fireplaces, original molding, hardwood floors, and an in-law suite for Bren, who makes her own soap. I just think that says a lot about a person. She gives me homemade soap almost every time I come to visit, and it's not because I smell.

The house they bought was for sale back when I was looking for a house here, but I passed on it because there was a crack house across the street, a drug dealer next door, and it was separated by only one street from Metropolitan Parkway, a crime-ridden corridor that has lately also become known for child prostitution. So from the beginning, Honnie and Todd picked a risky street even by Capitol View standards, but still, the entire house cost less than what a law partner would spend on a luxury car. Bummer about those addicts and all, but hey, when was the last time you saw a wrap-around porch at that price?

So Honnie and Todd bypassed the houses on the better streets because this house had high ceilings, those fabulous tiled fireplaces and, oh my God, that *kitchen*. You could host a seminar in that kitchen. My own kitchen counter is so small it couldn't support a card game, but theirs is bigger than the width of my entire bathroom. So Honnie and Todd bought the place, jumped on it. After that, I guess the first bad sign would have been the dead dog.

But Honnie did not take that as an omen. If the dead dog was a message from the drug dealers in the neighborhood, she surmised, then they would have thrown it on her doorstep and not just on her front yard. But looking back, you have to admit that having a dead dog tossed in your yard the day you move in is a bad sign. Then there was the crack house across the street.

"You cannot imagine the hassle it is to have a crack house on your block," Honnie tells me. But I think I can relate. I don't have a crack house on my block, but eight houses away from mine is the intersection known as "Crack Corner," where dealers congregate to make themselves available to addicts. They are constantly wandering into traffic, too, and I almost ran one down, which is how I got my nickname in the neighborhood. "Bleachy-haired honky bitch!" they've yelled at me since.

So I think I can relate, but I'm wrong. For example, Honnie tells me she was driving to work one morning and looked over to see a whore giving blow jobs to three men standing in line along the side of the crack house. So Honnie is right, I can't even imagine that. I didn't even know it was possible to give head to three men at once. Would you have to be like a performing seal, tooting on horns or something? What?

"Yeah, like that," Honnie says dryly. "What a great way to start the day." I didn't know if she meant her having to look at it or the whore having to do it, but I figured either was bad so I didn't press. I was there to sit vigil with her on her porch, so the dealer and drug addicts would know there was some neighborhood solidarity behind this kind couple and their mother. We actually had shifts. Mine was up when I saw Victoria walking up the path, her gait uneven and assisted by her cane. Victoria lives in the apartment complex on Metropolitan Parkway where, a few years ago, police found the bodies of a bridegroom and his best man on the day of their wedding ceremony. The two had come to partake in the strip joints along the Metropolitan Parkway corridor as part of a bachelor-party excursion and ended up dead. There are plenty of very bad people who live in that apartment complex, and plenty of good people, too.

Victoria ambles up to Honnie's porch and gives Honnie a hug. "Don't you worry," she tells us. "Ain't nobody gonna hurt nobody while I'm here."

MY *LAYOVER HOTEL,* it turns out, is only three blocks away from Sunset Boulevard, and the Whiskey-a-Go-Go is *right there*. The reason I'm bothered by this is that it took me three trips to figure it out.

I mean, the Hollywood I remember, barely, used to be seedy and dangerous. There would be no way you could stay at a fancy hotel three blocks away from Sunset with signs in the windows that read, "Please be respectful of our neighbors by keeping noise to a minimum." There would be no way you could be here three times and three blocks away from the Whiskey-a-Go-Go and not *know* it. You would have to be blind.

Historically, or in my personal history anyway, the Whisky-a-Go-Go is beyond riotous, beyond big. It's supposed to be surrounded by heroin addicts and other unwashed flotsam. There should *not* be a place to get a good cappuccino within walking distance. There should *not* be a swanky cafe with cloth-covered tables and a hostess podium on the sidewalk next door. But then again, I should not be here on business, either. Go figure.

But back to the Whiskey, it should be sort of sinister, I swear. You should be scared when you stand in line there, hoping to get a glimpse of some screeching urchin with grommets embedded in his head while you hop around in the crowd like a crushed pogo in a puddle of what you're hoping isn't someone else's piss.

I was there exactly once, when I was sixteen and lived in a suburb of Los Angeles called Torrance that seemed to be an entire solar system away from Sunset Boulevard. It seriously seemed like we had to cross the continental divide to reach Hollywood, when in fact Torrance is just a

We Were Blind

couple of freeway stops south, but to me it was the distance between my tepid existence and the mysterious frontier of all that is cool and bitchin'. To me it was galaxies away.

I would not have gone at all if not for the practical blindness that befell my parents during their divorce. It was as if giant cracks formed in their awareness, cracks through which I willingly fell. My mother had moved out of our apartment and then booted my Dad's ass out a few months later because she was tired of paying his rent. My sister and I stayed there alone, as my mother was loath to break her half-year lease on her place across town at the singles complex. So for that period between my father's moving out and my mother's neglecting to move back in, my little sister and I lived by ourselves with nothing but our own teenage brains to keep us in line. You can imagine the success of that situation.

Enter my best friend Kathy, who drove me to Hollywood at midnight in a Pinto completely void of headlights. I mean there were literally none, and even the encasements that would have housed them were gone, with nothing left but some fray-tipped colored wires dangling as if the Pinto's eyes had been plucked out in Oedipal fury. Kathy's family was experiencing something she considered similar to my own situation. Her recently divorced mother had begun seriously dating a Coast Guard employee, and Kathy's habit was to revolt so heinously in their presence that they were more grateful she was gone than worried where she'd be.

Sunset Boulevard was appropriately packed with prostitutes and crazy people back then, each flinching reflexively as Kathy and I drew near in our lightless Pinto. I'm guessing they'd had few positive experiences that involved a car approaching with its headlights out. But we were not looking for trouble, we were looking for a parking space.

At the Whiskey we danced until we physically damaged ourselves and those around us. To this day I don't know if I got into a fight that night or if all that punching and hair pulling was just part of the normal punk reverie. At one point a girl had a hold of my hair like it was the handle to my head, but I didn't take it person-ally, figuring it was my fault for wearing a ponytail to a punk-rock venue.

We'd been unsuccessful in our search for a parking space, so Kathy had pulled onto the lawn of an apartment complex nearby and that's where we'd left her car for the night. It could very well have been one of these residences right here across from my little boutique hotel, one of the places for whose benefit I am asked to keep quiet. Today this neighborhood is downright upscale. No wonder I didn't recognize it.

But for a second there last night, stopped at a light on the cor-ner of Sunset and San Vincente, it came back to me. I caught a flicker of the fashionable crustiness this place used to encase. I saw the two of us, Kathy and I, lost in the cracks, slicing through the night in complete darkness on our way to a place galaxies away. You'd be surprised at the distance you can cover in a car with its eyes gouged out, and the things you can get away with when peo-ple can't see you coming. That was us, careening through life like we had no idea we were blind.

YOU CANNOT FATHOM the crap I'm about to get from everyone for the following confession, so here it is. It turns out, after all that cocky posturing on my part, all that bloviating about how I am officially a member of the human-tripod league due to the Y chromosome growing in my gut, all that waving around of a sonogram picture that was supposed to have been *proof* that the linebacker in my belly is, indeed, a boy—not to mention the goddam *amnio* results, which are *error free*—after all of that it turns out *I don't have a penis after all*!

Jesus God! I should have known. I mean, I was itching to *braid hair*, and that's not like me at all. But I kept getting mental pictures of plastic barrettes and ribbons, and glittery little butterfly clips or whatever. I swear, this kid was headed for a hairdo so encrusted with cutesy little gadgets I could've used her head as a reflector to flag for help from the bottom of a well. So I was getting definite girl vibes from this baby all along. But a future mother's instinct isn't based in science like all those tests they put me through—tests in which bespectacled people poked at me like aliens inspecting an abducted bovine right before the farmer finds it dead in the field with its asshole missing—those tests are *scientific*.

So of course I believed them when they told me the results. But I should clarify myself here: the results were, in fact, accurate, but *science* doesn't take into consideration the human fallacy factor, and in this case that factor consisted of a nurse who was pregnant herself, *with a boy*. Evidently, at the precise moment in which she was telling me the sex of my future child, her brain burped out "boy" instead of "girl," thereby reducing these 100 percent sure-fire tests to a bunch of blathering snake-oil hokums that have all the accuracy of a blindfolded rooster pecking out winners on a racing form. Next time I might as well let my psychic friend Sherrie Cash rub bloody rabbit bladders on my belly, or whatever it is she does to determine the sex of the baby before it's born.

It's not like I'm picky about the gender of my baby. I had all those tests performed because I wanted to make sure the baby wasn't packing a basket of extra chromosomes or something, what with me being a hundred years old and my ovaries covered in cobwebs and all. Finding out the baby's sex was supposed to be a side perk. It was three months before they discovered their mistake. *Three months.* Three months of me calling the kid "Maxwell" and fighting with my friends over my decision not to circumcise.

And God! Was I cocky on the "clip" debate. Even though I was amazed at how hung up men could be on what other people's penises should look like, what really pissed me off were women! Women who felt compelled to impose on me their disgust over the unpruned. "It's gross," they'd squeal, as if they'd ever be in a position to have sex with my son. You know, I still say that not one of these girls, regardless of all that preening, would pass up a bout of bestial fornication because of an intact foreskin. So drop the irritating chastity act, okay?

But I digress. The point is this: when Michael used to tell me, "You have a lot to say for someone with no penis," *he was right*. I hate that he was right. Before, when he said this to me, I'd point to my sonogram to prove him wrong. But sonograms are like dental X-rays, you just look at where the doctor is pointing and think you see what is supposed to be there. In this case there was nothing there. *It was a shadow.* But don't get me wrong. I'm glad I'm having a girl. I hardly miss my penis at all, and now that everything's straightened out I can get back on track with my original maternal vibe, and that is to raise a daughter with plenty of balls.

THANK GOD CAR ACCIDENTS are behind me. Fourteen is enough, I tell you, whereas thirteen definitely was not. I remember when I'd had my thirteenth and thought, "Christ, I know I won't leave it at that," and right away I was worried, because I know me. I am so superstitious I even consider being superstitious to be bad luck.

For example, when I used to play tournament tennis as a kid, and I found myself losing the match (as I always did), I'd start throwing pieces of myself away. Seriously, I'd go to the back fence to collect the ball and toss my bracelet through the chain link, or necklace, or macramé belt, or *whatever*. Once I even took off my socks, tossed them. They all became evil talismans as the game wore on. They were black holes sucking all the luck out of me, and they had to be purged. Even my tennis shoes became cursed. When I tried to finish a match barefoot the club manager finally intervened.

I never won a match. I didn't even win a *concession* match, which were sort of side matches that tournament officials threw together to give all the losers of the real match something to do until the end of the event. Since none of my offerings to the angry tennis God were sufficient to garner me a single trophy, I concluded it was the superstitions themselves that were bad luck, so every time it even crept into my head that, for example, Ah ha! It's my wicked sweatband that's making me lose, I'd cringe like I was bracing for a blow, because right there I'd gone and blown it by being superstitious. So, you know, it all went inward. My own brain became the evil talisman.

So, at thirteen car wrecks, I was doubly cursed, because (1) it's impossible to avoid thinking that's a bad number to stand on, and (2) it really is a bad number to stand on. So I knew there was another wreck coming to me, and knowledge like that makes things uncomfortable, believe me.

I'd started having the wrecks at eighteen, and I don't even count the time my engine blew up as a wreck, or even as my fault, for that matter. When my sister Cheryl gave me her gold 1969 VW bug, she said these exact words, "The oil light is broken, that's why it keeps blinking." Even so, looking back I must say I was impressed that the car ran like that for about a month before the engine block finally cracked like a cantaloupe rind.

So of course I rebuilt it. The car went from being free to costing me five hundred dollars—or costing my mother that amount, anyway. She paid it out of guilt for having freshly left my father, who had a job selling used cars. That is how my sister got her hardly driven Toyota Celica, hence the VW bug hand-me-down.

After the divorce, my mother moved us to San Diego, and I intermittently made the two-hour commute to visit my father until two years later when he died. That last commute was when the car wrecks started—two in one day, mind you. First I was rear-ended on the freeway outside of San Clemente as I slowed for construction work, but the damage wasn't debilitating so we continued on. Then a lady *backed into* me at a stop light right outside my father's car lot, where my little sister Kim and I were headed to pick up my father's effects along with the proceeds from a modest life-insurance policy.

At eighteen, I was right to worry this was the beginning of something big. The first thing I did with the life-insurance check was buy a used 1974 Datsun 240Z, and the first thing I did with that was wreck it. So of course I rebuilt. Wreck. Repeat. Wreck. Repeat, until nine years later at number fourteen, which had been a 1963 Beetle, cherry in color and condition. But at fourteen I knew I was finished. "That's enough," I said to myself as I watched the tow truck drag away the shredded mess my car had become. I didn't even bother to rebuild it. There just comes a point when the damage around you matches the damage you feel inside, and you're finished with wrecking things.

Back when I'd gone with my sister to the car lot to pick up my father's stuff, his boss met us at the door. He looked to be, maybe, half my father's age. I realized then that, by the time my father had gotten this job, it had been nine years since he'd had one, and nine months after that my mother had left him.

At that point she packed us up and left him there with nothing but his new job selling cars, but at least he could drive a different model every day to help take his mind off the rubble his marriage had become. At least there was that, right?

"Can I interest you in a used car?" our father's boss cracked as he directed me to my dad's desk. Then he saw my face. "Bad joke," he muttered, disappearing only to lurk as car salesmen do sometimes, like oil seeping into sand. My parents had been married longer than the life of my father's boss, I realized then. Wreck. Repeat. Wreck. Repeat. Wreck. Repeat, until twenty-five years later, when the damage around them matched the damage they felt inside, and they didn't bother to rebuild.

LARY SAYS I'M LUCKY my body is not buried in a hole in his basement right now. If he'd hesitated at all before shooting at me that one time, he might have aimed better and actually hit me and I'd be dead right now "in a big way," he says. But because he didn't hesitate, *at all*, and just grabbed the gun and shot at me in one fluid motion, the bullet harmlessly ricocheted off a rock and landed in a plant bed.

"That is why you're alive today," he says, "because I didn't hesitate."

"That is crap," I say. Not only do I think he should have hesitated a little, I still strongly believe he should not have shot at me at all, even though I was breaking into his house at the time. He has since given me a new key.

You'd think that, since I'm good at breaking into cars, I'd have a natural talent for houses, too, but I don't. In fact, if ever I need to break into a house I just call Lary, and he shows up in a truck. I don't even know how he does it (maybe I should take notes); all I know is that, with him there, what was once locked is now not. He doesn't seem to have any special tools that I can see. He just tells me to wait outside the front door, and soon he is opening it from the other side for me. "How did you get in?" I ask.

"It was easy," is all he says.

He once helped me break into Daniel's place because I ran out of margarita mix, and tequila, too, and while I was there I might as well take that melon liqueur, and . . . oh, what the hell, why lug it all back across the hall to my place when I can mix it all right here in Daniel's vintage Osterizer? He won't mind. A few months prior he and Grant broke into my place and ate all the chocolate reindeer out of the Christmas baskets I used to make for my supervisors back when I thought kissing ass mattered in my business, and a few months before that they broke in while I was actually there, sleeping off a bender. They littered my whole house with condom wrappers and then the next morning tried to tell me that I stumbled home in a drunken stupor and pulled a train on a bunch of Mexican busboys.

So I don't want to dig a hole for myself here, but what good is a friend if you can't break into his damn house? Lary's been my friend longer than anyone practically, and half the fun of having friends is invading their territory. Up until Lary shot at me I was routinely plundering through his personal stuff looking for nude self-Polaroids he might use to solicit sex on the Internet or something. I swear, I could not believe that man wasn't hiding something, I even looked under the tarps in his backyard, but all I found were a couple of car carcasses and a litter of thin, feral kittens.

"If you didn't change your locks, I wouldn't have needed to break in," I remind him, which is true. Up until then I'd had my own personal key to Lary's door, which he had personally given me. Then he just up and changed his locks one day, which I think is very inconsiderate, and then to shoot at me for doing what I had no choice but to do? That is downright rude.

"What's rude is I almost had to bury you in my basement," Lary bitches. "Think of the hole I almost had to dig!"

I was ten the first time I broke into a house—with my older sister, who was in middle school and therefore more attuned to the criminal mind. She had somehow procured the key to the house of a twelve-year-old boy named Tyler, with whom we were both in love. He had curly dark hair past his shoulder blades and wore low-slung jeans anchored by a belt buckle in the shape of a big metal skull with a snake all wound up in the eye sockets.

My sister Cheryl didn't know that I was also in love with Tyler; I kept that part secret because I was afraid she wouldn't let me help her break into his house if she knew, and I was absolutely atwitter with anticipation. I swear, I think I even talked myself into believing I would find rough drafts of love letters written to me, all aching with longing and revealing a sensitivity very advanced for an adolescent. I even had him lusting after the curve of my neck in those letters, I think, wanting to engulf my clavicle with kisses and whatnot.

This is all due to the fact that I'd stolen romance novels from my mother's bedside and read in secret the travails of many an Edwardian beauty. In these books, the heroine always very romantically fell in love with her first lover, who was very ardent, tender, and vulnerable for a rapist. The curve of her neck always seemed to be the thing that sent the nobleman masquerading as a commoner into the throes of mad passion, crumbling the façade of his blue-blooded upbringing and releasing the beast within. After that they'd inevitably become awash in an unfathomable ocean of desire, with yearning breasts bursting and a big throbbing python of love.

Stuff like this is irresistible to a ten-year-old, and I was always thrusting my neck out at Tyler, wondering how he could resist the yearning breasts bursting beneath my tank top. When I heard my sister planned to break into his house I stuck to her like putty until she agreed I could come. We picked Saturday in broad daylight to pull it off. I wore garden gloves to mask my fingerprints, which was unnecessary, because I was soon sent to the kitchen for look-out duty while my sister alone got to wallow in Tyler's stuff.

I was quite bored in the kitchen until I opened a drawer located under the wall-mounted telephone and found a deck of pornographic playing cards. The queen of hearts held particular interest for me, since she literally had a throbbing python of love in every orifice, plus one in each fist. *Jesus God*, I thought, *she's all plugged up.*

She did not look like she was awash in an unfathomable ocean of desire. She just looked incredibly uncomfortable. Just then my sister emerged from Tyler's bedroom, and in her hand she gripped his big belt buckle. She planned to treasure it for the rest of her life, she said, wadded up in her pajama top as she slept, even. But when we got home, I stole that belt buckle back from her and buried it behind a briar bush in our backyard. It was quite an effort to dig that hole, too, I tell you, because I had to make it big enough to fit all my mother's romance novels as well.

I **DID NOT START THE RUMOR** that Grant and Matt slept together. *Grant* started that rumor. I swear, according to him, he and Matt have practically been stuck together like sucker fish since 1997, barring that prison stint Matt had to complete a couple of years ago owing to all those banks he robbed in his early twenties.

Anyway, it's not *my* fault Matt's now all in love with someone else and has some answering to do. I hear she is very pretty, Matt's new love, but then Grant's the one who told me that. I believe him, though, because Matt himself is very pretty and it just seems appropriate to bookend him with the same. Sometimes I can just look at Matt for whole minutes on end and wonder how someone with eyes as big and blue as two planet Plutos right there on his face—and that *face*, Michelangelo could not have carved such a beautiful face—how someone with a face like that could fuck Grant and rob banks, not that he did both at the same time or either at all (though the bank robbing is actually documented by a formal confession). And that's not even counting the addictions.

"I have a very addictive personality," Matt told me once. He was sitting across from me in a booth at the Local, his face just as sweet as Easter candy. His proclamation surprised me. This "addictive personality" was news. "Does Matt really have an addictive personality?" I asked Grant later.

"Well, there was the heroin," he said, "and the sex, and, you know, the bank robbing," he continued, "so, yeah."

Heroin? Where the hell did that come from? I swear, you think you know somebody . . . and then sometimes you do know somebody, but you just don't want to know everything. For example, when I was seventeen I ended up sleeping with a heroin addict who was every bit as beautiful as Matt. His name was Scott, and he was a surfer boy who graduated from my high school before I started my freshman year, but all the students still talked about him like he was still around.

He wasn't, not in any sense. Not then, anyway. I met him through my sister, who dated his roommate, and I don't know why Scott set his sights on me when there were so many walking bikini stuffers he could ball, why he centered in on this awkward high-school kid with hardly any friends, but I think maybe my youthful incorruptibility might have been a factor. There is just something about a new book that makes you want to flip through the pages and bend the bindings back, isn't there?

Anyway, that must have been something he couldn't stand to not destroy, the newness of me, because he always acted kind of crazed when I was around, like I was an overly frosted birthday cake and him there with his finger just out of reach. To my dubious credit I kept myself out there for years before I finally let him reach me. By then he was recovering from his addiction, as well as a hellacious, half-year-long bout of hepatitis, and my sister had moved on to another boyfriend, a fry cook at the coffee shop where she waitressed. I don't even remember how it happened, how one day I was incorruptible and the next I was not; the memory has been banished from my brain like bad bacteria. I just know it had something to do with love.

Not love for Scott, hell no. I was stupid in love with another boy, who made use of me until my usefulness turned into burden, I suppose. He was the bag boy at the local grocer down the street from my house, and I craved him like I was suffocating and his breath was my only salvation. I swear if it were up to my mindset at the time, I would still, to this day, be spending every afternoon the same, waiting by the window in front of my house to see him drive by after his shift in his flawlessly preserved 1963 red VW Bug. Sometimes he was coming to get me and other times he just passed me by. It was there, in front of my house in the front seat of that Bug, that this boy informed me of the burden I'd become, and afterward he had to physically pull me out of the passenger side as I clung to him, unwilling to let go of my jones. "I'll change," I begged, but he was already gone.

From there Scott plucked me up like a berry from a bush. It was that easy. I allowed him to corrupt me in many imaginative ways, all the while hoping the bag boy would intervene. But when Scott started shooting up again, he did not try to take me there, I have to give him that. He hid it from me until I found him in my bathroom one night, the needle already in his arm. Maybe he was hoping I'd intervene, too, I don't know. It's funny with addictive personalities, because they don't just want what they can take, they want what they can't reach as well. So it's not surprising to remember how long Scott stayed in my life in all, with both of us wanting something we couldn't reach.

COULDN'T SLEEP LAST NIGHT because, among other things, I was kept awake by the thought of what a bad mother I'll probably make. And by the way, am I going to give birth to this baby out my *ass*? Because that's where I'm gaining all my weight. Is this normal? I feel like a walking trash bag full of pig fat. My future kid will be ashamed of me when I drop her off at kindergarten. Not only that, the sonograms keep showing a critter with a huge head.

And do they make cribs you can suspend from the ceiling? Because my house has reached maximum crap capacity now that I don't throw everything away anymore. Not only that, since I painted this whole place before I knew the fumes could be harmful, I'm scared that now my baby will be born inside out or something, with organs flopping off it like fleshy little saddlebags. If that happens, Lary says, at least we can sell it for parts. "You would probably get more for it that way than if you sold it all in one piece," he says.

I've learned that sometimes Lary is not the person to go to when I'm anxious, so notice how I haven't been calling him a lot lately. I guess he's afraid I'm gonna storm his house with my big-headed baby and lactate on him or something. Like I would *ever* bring a baby to Lary's house, especially a big-headed baby, because he lives in an alleyway with tools and torches strewn about, and he might as well have a sign above the door that reads "Lary's lair of sharp edges and fire."

But keeping my kid from Lary's place is about the extent of my maternal instincts. Looking back at my own childhood I'm surprised I survived. My mother made *bombs*, for chrissakes. As a missile scientist you would think she'd experiment beyond our two family food groups—Hawaiian Punch and Halloween candy—but no, so by the time I was ten I had such a permanent sugar buzz I could register on the Richter scale. And my father was an alcoholic trailer salesman who liked to drive drunk with me in the front seat. Once he ran over a lady's foot, but that's because she deserved it, he said. For family entertainment we used to cruise through the cemetery and watch the deer eat flowers off of fresh graves.

I grew up thinking all this was normal.

This is not normal. But still, at family gatherings we used to laugh so hard it felt like our lungs would collapse. In the end, I think the only thing my parents really did wrong was not live long. Once, when I was studying literature in England at Oxford, my mother sent me a letter saying how proud she was. Of me. The letter was long and full of things I need to hear right now, but I was really young and thought my mother was as invincible as I was, and I used to have this bad habit of throwing everything away. So the letter is gone, and another reason I can't sleep at night is because I stay awake trying to recall everything it said. I think if I concentrate hard enough I can hear my mother's voice, and sometimes I do. She talks about my resolve, my determination, my ability to conquer things, and she says something else that wasn't in the letter; advice good enough to pass onto my child. She says, "Don't throw everything away."

LARY IS MAKING A LIST of his fears. "What the hell for?" I ask. "So I can do 'em all," he says, and I have to laugh at that. God knows Lary has no fears that are easily faceable. Like he has no fear of skydiving or death or snakes or Satan or any other basic fright that strikes ice into the hearts of normal people. His biggest fear is living in a duplex on Chipmunk Lane in Lilburn, Georgia. His biggest fear is being surrounded by mid-income soccer moms who will insist he clean all the decayed auto parts off his driveway and who will call the police when he puts an old refrigerator in his front yard with a sign that says, "Great Playhouse."

"What're you gonna do? Move to a suburban cul-de-sac?" I ask.

"A fear is something that has a possibility of happening," he jibbers, backpedaling. "I don't care what happens or how good looking the girl is, I'll never wake up on Chipmunk Lane."

We are at the Local, and Keiger won't front him a free dinner, even though I personally told Lary it was on the house. "Order anything you want," I said magnanimously, because lately I've taken to telling customers there that their tab is on the house, even though I don't own the place or have any right to give anything away. Keiger does own it, though, and it pleases me to see him swoop in after me and make people pay anyway. Before he bought this bar, Keiger parked cars for a living, and he's said he has a fear of ending up back there again. So to help him out I offer to ease his way into bankruptcy, because I think it's important to face your fears, but so far Keiger is not on board with this. He keeps making people pay anyway.

I personally have a fear of ending up in a

trailer on a homestead in the middle of some dismal expanse of land. Like Keiger and his fear, I have experienced mine and don't want to go back. For a long period after my parents divorced, I lived with my mother in a trailer two miles north of the Tijuana border, and I still haven't decided if it was as bad as you might think. There was a clubhouse, for example, and monthly "mixers," during which the trailer-park residents mingled over coffee and home-baked cinnamon cake. There were a lot of old people with missing limbs living there, too, and they seemed eager for company.

Our trailer itself wasn't so bad, either. There was carpeting on the floor and blankets on the beds. But the front door was about as substantial as one you'd find on a kitchen cupboard in a real house, and every step you took in the place made it shake like a boxcar, a constant and unwelcome testimony to its impermanence.

I remember there was a collective effort on the part of the trailer owners to pretty up their lots. Most of the trailers had permanent-ish porches that were fashioned to provide access to the front door as though you were walking up to a real home as opposed to one on wheels, and the wheels themselves were often hidden by lattice fencing surrounding the underside of the trailer. But in my eyes all these efforts couldn't belie that this place was little more than a shantytown.

The black widow didn't help, either. I don't have a fear of spiders in general, just poisonous ones in particular, and it seriously did not help that a big black widow lived in the storage shed in back of my mother's trailer. I was constantly needing to get into that shed, too, because that is where most of my important stuff ended up, stuff like the one-eyed snake I won at a carnival when I was seven. There was not a lot of room in my mother's trailer for these treasured items, so they were all relegated to the shed and guarded by the black widow, which lived at knee level just inside the door.

My practice was to simply open the door of the shed and sit

there, wailing and pointing at it, which one day caused my heavy-set neighbor, Tillie, to shout at me. She was sitting in her wheel-chair on her porch one day as I did this. "What the hell is wrong with you?" she hollered.

I told her about the poisonous spider and how, even if I stuck my hand in the shed on the whole other side away from the black widow, I might snag a piece of the web, therefore triggering the spider to somehow career up onto my head and bite me on my brain.

Tillie had just had her legs amputated due to diabetes, and their bandaged stumps stuck out from beneath her large body like two big broken broomsticks. "Goddammit, girl, you've got feet, right? I ain't got feet, but you do, right? Well, then, look at your foot and then look at the spider. Your foot is bigger, isn't it? You're a lot bigger. Now just stomp on that damn spider and shut the hell up."

So I did as she said. I stomped on it, and to this day I continue to take Tillie's advice any time I can. It was sage wisdom, after all. In the end, we are all bigger than our fears. We should all just stomp on them and shut the hell up.

I'S TOO BAD testicles are such an easy target. Really. And they always seem to be hanging there at table-corner height, which just makes them cumbersome. But to have them shot off, that right there is the motherfuck of all motherfucks, if you ask me, even though you could argue I have none of my own anymore—balls, that is.

That police deputy did, though, poor guy. He and his partner were just doing their job in my neighborhood, visiting from their own district, serving what they considered to be a low-risk warrant on Jamil Abdullah Al-Amin, a Muslim cleric who is supposed to be a pillar of our community, and for some reason Al-Amin pulled out an assault rifle and shot them both. Then while they lay there in the street wounded, Al-Amin slowly approached one and shot his balls off, three bullets to the groin, which killed him fairly efficiently, while the other deputy watched, horrified.

The next day I knew something was up in my neighborhood the second I turned the corner past the crack dealers and saw immediately that our regular contingent of whores were nowhere to be seen, especially Pox Face, who was probably the most visible hooker we had. That was not her actual name, just one I'd given her. I've only seen her through my car window, and she was so ugly I wondered whether the reason she was so reliably on the street was because she had a hard time getting any business, an assumption backed by her lack of shoes.

Pox Face used to wear an old pair of riding boots I'd picked up at a thrift store as part of a failed Halloween costume a few years back. I was going to be an old-fashioned stewardess, and the closest thing I could find to the kind of go-go boots they used to wear back in the good old days—back when Pucci designed the uniforms and everybody belted shots in the cockpit—were these lame riding boots. So I bought them, figuring I could paint them white, but thankfully ditched the idea. The boots, though, stayed with me until I moved to Capitol View.

It is the practice of me and my neighbors to leave useable items we no longer want on top of the lid of our trash containers the day trash is to be collected, seeing as how there are so many needy people in the neighborhood, and it takes probably ten minutes, tops, before the item is picked up and disbursed among the miscreants who populate this place. Those boots, though, must have stayed out there for hours. I was really surprised. I thought they'd go fast, even though they're a size ten. Finally they got picked up by Pox Face, and she wore them until she lost them, because crack whores lose everything eventually. Every little thing.

But none of the whores were visible the morning after Al-Amin shot the balls off that deputy. What I did see, though, were police cars. I never saw so many police cars on Dill Avenue. The crack dealers were there, too. You can't let a little cop killing get in the way of commerce, I guess.

Al-Amin is on the run right now, that's why the police are canvassing our neighborhood. They believe he has a lot of supporters here, and he does. The Muslim population in our neighborhood is collectively aghast. They are insisting Al-Amin is innocent, a bastion of our community, and crediting him with having cleaned up the West End where we live. "He swept this place up," they insist. If he is persecuted and put to death, they say, our neighborhood will be sentenced to death as well.

Now I'm not black and I'm not Muslim—not that I know of anyway, because the truth is both of my parents died before I started caring about heritage, thus making it hard for me to harangue them for information—but I am a resident of the community Al-Amin is credited with cleaning up, and I can tell you truthfully the man sucks as a housekeeper. First of all, leaving dead policemen lying around with their balls shot off is damn fucking messy. But besides that even, I have never once seen Al-Amin come by with his big broom to sweep up the dealers on Crack Corner down the street from my house, or to sweep up the pimps who peddle child prostitutes on Metropolitan Parkway, or even to help Honnie and Todd, who have been terrorized and shot at by the drug dealer next door since soon after they moved in. A lot of people in the neighborhood came forth to help them, to sit on their porch with them and hold vigil with them in a show of support. None of them were assault-rifle toting pillars, granted, but they did what they could. Where was Al-Amin then?

Maybe he was busy. I guess it takes time to stockpile weapons and plan a botched double cop killing, where you blast the balls off of one and leave the other lying there, looking at you, able to perfectly describe you plus the car you were driving. I guess it takes time to take stock in yourself, see that you have no balls, that you are just as nutless as the man you left dead in the street, then to run away and hide behind the faded faith of your neighbors.

I AM NOT DEAD, though there are ants in my bed, which blows my theory—I always thought you had to be dead before ants tried to eat you. I thought there was some kind of insect protocol when it came to insects and humans. Surely they don't eat you *alive*, do they? Don't forensic scientists use insect-feeding patterns as evidence to determine time of death?

I wouldn't be wondering this if I didn't live in a goddam peat bog. I swear, there must be a complete cosmic funnel through which all the spiders, ants, moths, and billion-legged robo-bugs in the world are sucked, and then there is my house, right under the butt end of the funnel, getting continuously crapped upon.

You'd think *walls* would make a difference, but they don't. I had better protection when I was living in a tent, even though I never really lived in one except for that week I went whitewater rafting in Colorado. My little sister lived in a tent, though, actually *lived* there with her husband Eddie. She said it was nice, with interior tent walls that divided it into separate rooms.

When I think of my sister's tent I think of Richard Burton in *Cleopatra*, when his army made "camp" before going into battle. Only Richard Burton's tent was like a mansion, with massive candelabras and gilded door-frames. *Doorframes*, in a *tent*. There weren't even doors, but there were red velvet drapes tied to the side with gold-tasseled cord. His bed, though, is what really cracked me up. It was an ornate, four-poster colossus, with about fifty pillows. That was a stupid-ass way to portray a Roman about to go into battle, but back when my sister told me she was living in a tent, I liked to think of the one Richard Burton had. "It's nice," she told me, and I really wanted to believe her.

Because what else was I gonna do? She was living in Zurich at the time, and I couldn't fly there from California to save her, especially since she didn't want to be saved. I'd already tried talking her out of marrying Eddie a year earlier, and all that did was build a wall between us. We'd started out living in Zurich together, along with my mother who'd been contracted to design weapons for the Swiss government. When the contract expired, I tried to get Kim to come home to the States with me, explaining, with all the gentleness of an angry bobcat, that she'd be a fool to stay. "Alcoholic walrus," for example, is what I called the man she loved. I blamed him for everything, too. I especially blamed him for the tent.

I didn't expect her to turn me down. Kim and I had been roommates in college. She kept the place clean and made sure the bills were paid, and in return I kept my cadre of meaningless boyfriends down to basic parade level. It was a great setup, if you ask me. It just seemed natural that my sister and I would emerge from the mended shipwreck that made up our childhoods to have a home in the same place. In my mind she would always be there, being my little sister, believing everything I said. I remember when her dimpled fingers used to be too short to reach the bottom of a bag of candy, so I'd tell her the candy was gone and finish the bag myself. I remember accepting money from my mother for teaching her how to read when, really, she'd already learned on her own somehow. I remember having dreams in which she was horribly hurt and waking with inconsolable sobs. I still have those dreams. Those don't go away.

Now here she was living in a tent and telling me it was nice. Sometimes I was fine with it. Sometimes I could put the thought of my homeless-but-for-a-tent little sister into a special compartment in my head and keep her there for long periods. "She says it's nice," I'd tell myself.

But other times I'd let it hit me with the dull thump of dead birds. Jesus God, this was my little sister, living in a tent halfway across the hemisphere, and in the end I left her there. I cannot believe I left her there. To this day I still don't know what is best; to sit a world away while your little sister lives in a tent and do nothing but buffer your worry with walls you build in your brain, or to drop everything and make your way back to her, so that you can take her dimpled hand and bring her home. All I know is this: her home and my home had become two separate places, with walls all their own, and she knew that before I did.

She is no longer living in a tent, thank God. She lives in a nice house with real walls now, in Dayton, Ohio, of all places, with her husband Eddie, a big dreamer whom I've grown to love. We had our walls up, yes we did, my sister and I, but eventually our devotion returned. It made its way in, seeping through the cracks like insects, and after enough of that the walls weakened and we loved each other again, or we were brave enough to let each other know we never stopped.

IF MY MOTHER HAD BEEN A BETTER THIEF, I would not be here right now. Not that she wasn't skilled, mind you, she was. I'd even say she was better than Lary, who right now is the best klepto I know. But Lary relies on the obvious. For example, he will simply walk into the waiting room of an upscale plastic surgeon's office with a hand truck and take the leather couch right out from under the newly lipo-sucked asses of the patients there. "Move aside," he'd say. "Emergency couch removal." Nobody would stop him because such a blatant theft is outside their sphere of experience. In short, they'd believe him because believing him would be so much more comfortable than confronting him.

My mother, too, occasionally used that technique—like once she stole all the patio furniture from the poolside of the condo complex where she used to reside by simply backing a borrowed truck up to the gate and loading up—but she didn't rely on it. Her expertise was much more refined. She had great sleight of hand. She could steal from *casinos*, for chrissakes. I cannot overemphasize the skill factor there, the dexterity you'd need to steal stuff off the top of a casino blackjack table. With that talent she could have performed her own show on one of Las Vegas's lesser stages, say the Hoe-Daddy room at downtown's Binion's Horseshoe as opposed to the blow-ass velvet-curtain faux-Broadway number at the Venetian on the strip.

She took things from her office, too, and not just the industrial big blocks of Post-it notes, either, but outdated classified documents detailing projects she had been working on. She gave them to me once so I could present them as my own when I applied for a job as a technical writer for a company in Zurich that made corrugated materials. I was not qualified to be a technical writer for a cardboard-box company, especially a German-speaking company, but here we were living in Switzerland because my mother had scored work designing missiles for the Swiss government, and she wasn't about to let a little thing like national security get in the way when I decided I wanted a job of my own. It wasn't *America's* national security, after all, just Switzerland's.

Besides, she was always talking about how none of the stuff she designed for them ever seemed to work properly. Take the time she traveled to a Sardinian testing facility to trial the missile tracking device she helped design. The purpose of the weapon was to intercept enemy missiles and facilitate their destruction before they reached their target. It was a precursor to the Patriot missiles that are used in Iraq today, with the exception that her device didn't work.

"It just fell the hell over," she laughed afterward. "It fell right off its base and onto the goddam ground."

So she stole those documents for those weapons and tried to get me to pass them off as my own, because a place that makes cardboard boxes surely could use a technical writer astute enough to build her own bomb, right? "Hell, yes," she said, "get out there."

Because here's the thing: I was leaving and she knew it. I'd had enough of Switzerland and rich people and goddam fondue and humorlessness in general, which is how I viewed the country overall. I'd been there a year and a half, since I graduated from college, living there with my brilliant mother as she designed worthless weapons for a pussy-ass country known for its neutrality, and I was *bored*. I wanted my own job, I wanted to make my own damn way, and every Thursday I'd scan the *International Herald Tribune* classifieds and find companies throughout Europe looking for people to fill positions I figured I could passably fake my way into pulling off.

Unlike my mother, I did not have a contract keeping me in Zurich, and she could see me standing there at the ready, with one foot in her world and the other poised over the goddam banana peel that would make up the rest of my life, and if she wanted to she could have stolen that from me. She could have put her own foot down or gone ballistic or threatened all kinds of untold emotional tortures only mothers can administer when their children threaten to forge away from them, or she could have simply told me the truth about how seriously sick she really was, about how little life she herself had left, and it would have been so easy for her to steal mine from me.

But she didn't. She let me go. I left her in Zurich alone to finish her contract while I flew back to the States, where I proceeded over the next decade to consistently fall on my ass until finally I ended up where I belong. It could have been different, believe me. Right now I could be sitting here with a sack of broken dreams, a bitter bag of fears, wearing a badge on a lanyard around my neck, a technical writer, maybe, for a company that makes cardboard boxes. That's where I'd be if my mother had been a better thief.

STILL HAVE A PICTURE on my refrigerator of Grant and Daniel dressed as cowgirls. I think everyone should have a picture like this somewhere prominent in their house, of two total fairies trapped in their adolescence. They each have enough makeup on their faces to fill a bucket, and fake boobs so big they could float a houseboat.

I made their costumes myself, complete with yards of thick gold upholstery fringe I found at a salvage store. I actually sewed lassos and horse-shaped appliqués on their back pockets, too. It was good homemaking-type practice, seeing as how I used this same picture to adorn the invitations I sent for the baby shower these two supposedly threw for me.

I say "supposedly" because they hardly lifted a single bangle-weighted wrist to help me set up, and instead spent the whole pre-party prep time in Daniel's bathroom drinking mimosas and drenching each other in cosmetics. When they emerged, they were both dressed as pregnant country-singing queens, ready for the party to start, while my authentically two-hundred-month pregnant ass was still busy preparing appetizer trays.

"Can you two at least *pretend* like you're putting this party on and help?" I asked, but they waved me away, or maybe they were just waving in general, mindful as they were of their wet nail polish. Grant would not even so much as rinse off a cluster of grapes for me. I swear, sometimes I can see the true benefit behind having real females for girlfriends.

In the end I rolled up my sleeves, lumbered forth, and finished on my own. The result was a buffet and wine bar fit for a fleet of conquering Huns. It's a good thing, too, because about five hundred people showed up, everyone laden with gaily wrapped baby-type presents. When I finished tearing into them all, there was enough ribbon and paper strewn about to fully stuff a plush toy the size of a Trojan horse.

And you would not have believed the baby booty. That alone is reason to see the true benefit behind having your baby shower fronted by two bossy fags, because they both nagged the hell out of me to register a wish list at a sprogette shop, then they pestered everyone invited to the party to pay attention to it, which everyone did. Later I heard from the saleslady there that she had to add things to the list to accommodate requests. "You didn't have receiving blankets on the list, and you're gonna need those."

What the hell is a receiving blanket? I thought. In fact, I didn't know what the hell more than half the stuff was I'd been told I'd need. I put it on the list, though, and sure enough I got it handed to me wrapped in pastel-colored paper on the day of my shower. It was like magic. It took two cars and Lary's old truck bed (minus the portion used up by the big wad of barbed wired) to haul it all back to my place, where I sat among it all like Jabba the Hut, wondering what to do with it. It was all very intimidating. For example, what are nipple shields? I was told I'd need them, and here I had them, and I don't know what to do with them.

It was kind of like when I got my first ten-speed as a twelve-year-old. It was when my mother had been gainfully employed working with NASA on the last Apollo moon launch, so she had income then, as opposed to one Christmas a few years prior when she was between contracts and had to rely on charity to fill out the empty space under our tree. I guess to make up for that particular Christmas she went and bought me the biggest blow-ass ten-speed you ever saw, a top-of-the-line Schwinn with enough gears and googlydobs to run an efficient Swiss railway system.

The trouble was I had no idea how to work it. I literally used to just walk it to school every day, because I did not know even the first move to make to get it out of second gear, and my mother, an actual rocket scientist, was no help.

So I kept walking it to school, because, believe me, the bike garnered a hell of a lot of admiration from the other kids, particularly the boys, who would whistle at it like they were little construction workers and my bike was a big-chested blond. Normally they were like a swarm, these boys, all tormenting and daunting. It was all very intimidating. But the bike changed things. They'd ask to ride it, and I'd let them, because I figured if I'd insert the bike into their circle, everything would work. It was like adding a necessary mechanism to a complicated machine, and once all the parts were in place it ran flawlessly.

But all this baby booty, it was worse than a complicated bike. Once I got it home it all lay strewn about like a disassembled appliance. Breast pumps and bottle sterilizers, bassinettes and cradle bumpers, how do you work this stuff?

"Don't worry," my friend Jill told me. "The baby changes things. It's like the baby is the battery that fits into all the stuff and makes it work." Yes, that's it, she promised me. I'll have my daughter and, in a very big way—in wonderful ways I could not even imagine—she'll fit into all my stuff and make it work.

MY COMPUTER HAS BEEN INFECTED by so many viruses I finally had to quarantine it to the corner of my house, where it sits to this day, surrounded by flares so no one will go near it. It's truly evil, that computer, but I'm afraid to throw it away because it has stuff in there I need, like downloads of Grant's face superimposed on the body of a fat masturbating lady.

I don't know how to get that picture from my old computer to my new one, because I've converted to Macintosh, you know. Yes, I've got this new, sleek thing here that I can practically put in my pocket. Unlike my PC, it's not polluted inside, its cogs and inner workings aren't all crud covered, and when I turn it on it doesn't sound like I'm trying to start up a rusty lawnmower.

My only beef is the color. It's not just white, but *white* white, and I'm 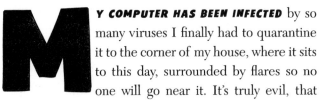 uncomfortable around so much purity. Lary says I should take black markers and just soil the thing once and for all, but I can't bring myself to do it. I have a hard enough time just witnessing the natural erosion of things.

Take the car I bought when I was eighteen, the sleek Datsun 240Z I paid for with what was left of my share of my father's, company-paid life insurance policy after I finished blowing half of it on cocaine for the gaggle of backstabbing assholes that made up most of my friends back then. Jesus God, that car was gorgeous, as blue as the color of a prom queen's eyes, with white racing stripes. I bought the car used, with ninety thousand miles on it, but to me it was as pure as Play-Doh fresh from the can. Within weeks I totaled it on the San Diego Freeway. The nice man I'd rear-ended gave me a ride home after they towed my wreckage away, as his huge Ford fuck-you mobile hardly sustained a scratch from the accident.

"That's right," he said, pounding his dashboard, "this here is American made. Nothin' better."

My father would have agreed with him, as when he died he'd had that job selling used cars. Every single one of them was American made. At his office a week after the funeral, when my father's supervisor handed the checks to my sister and me, I noticed a poster taped over his desk that read, "Believe = Achieve."

Outside it was raining those big, fat, heavy raindrops that actually hurt when they hit your head. After getting into our second accident that day, we drove two hours home in that, not saying much to each other, but thinking a lot nonetheless.

I was thinking of the time my father caught me in bed with Scott, that handsome heroin addict who would mark the first in a total toilet spin of awful men in my life. It was during the period when my younger sister and I were left to live on our own for a while, not that our parents didn't check in on us occasionally.

That's how I was busted in bed with Scott. My father had broken the law by opening the unlocked sliding-glass door of his former home and letting himself inside. Scott and I were asleep in his former bed, but I've always been a light sleeper, and I bounded up just as my father walked into the room. Thank God I had on pajamas.

"Dad," I exclaimed, taking him by the arm and leading him back out to the living room, "what are you doing here?"

"I came to check on you," he said.

I had it in my head that maybe my father didn't get a good look at Scott, who still slept obliviously in the bedroom. Maybe, since Scott had long blond hair, I could get out of this by telling my Dad it was my friend Kathy who came to spend the night, and we both just fell asleep innocently while watching TV in his bedroom. Yeah, that's it. He'll believe that.

"Of course I believe you," he said softly, and I could hardly fathom this was the same man who beat the crap out of me four years earlier just because I accidentally accepted a *Roe v. Wade* pamphlet from an activist.

I was relieved to have evaded a scene, but I still remember my father's face; it was the face of a man witnessing the erosion of things all around him—his marriage, his health, his daughter's purity—all of life's natural erosions that you can't do a damn thing about, but you tend to fight them anyway. Then the day comes when you catch your kid in bed with a boy, and that is the day you give up.

"Don't leave the sliding-glass door open anymore," my father said before leaving. "It's dangerous. You can get into all kinds of trouble." At that he closed the door quietly, and left his life behind.

My Pile

'D BE THE BIGGEST KLEPTO of all time if not for the fact that I'm afraid of getting crapped on by the karma gods. This is especially painful to admit since I hate the whole concept of karma. Seriously. I believe you should do good things simply because you're a good person, not because, ultimately, you have your own damn agenda in mind.

Not that I'm all that good of a person, but still I can't comfortably fit thievery into my life, otherwise I'd have a *pile*, I tell you. My own mother was a master thief. Consider the famous incident in which she stole a six-deck card shoe off the top of a blackjack table in Las Vegas. But truly, what fun is a card shoe? Even if it comes with the chain still attached, at best it's just something you can swing across the room and hit your sister in the head with. Other than that it has no use.

It still irks me that my mother never stole useful things. No. She only stole stuff she thought people wouldn't miss, like pool cues, ashtrays, hospital gowns, patio furniture, fireplace mantles, and so on. We had piles of this stuff, and I constantly lamented that my mother was not the kind of klepto who came home with watches and earrings and other practical items.

I found this out when I tried to place an order. I wasn't even being all that demanding, I thought. It seemed simple enough to me, to walk into a toy store and steal a trampoline, especially since my mother had recently come home with a one hundred-pound potted tree she took from a local hotel lobby, but that day I learned there's some kind of inner code among kleptos; they actually don't consider themselves thieves.

"I don't *steal*," my mother gasped, angrily grinding her spent menthol into an ashtray printed with the tiger and little Negro logo of a

Sambo's coffee shop. "If you want a brand-new trampoline you have to pay for it your own goddam self."

Paying for it myself meant hours of door-to-door cupcake sales, during which I usually ate half my inventory. I also tried to sell caramel apples and blond brownies, but they weren't as easy to push. There is just something about a cupcake being sold by a grade-schooler that sends housewives running for their wallets. If you tell them there's a purpose to the sales, that's even better.

I had some great stories for why I was selling cupcakes, too, all culled from conversations I'd overheard coming from my parents' bedroom, like the one about how I had to help pay for my brother's education so he could get a college degree and do all the things my father never got to do. Or the one about how my sister lost her shoes at the park and our family was gonna have to live in the gutter if we had to keep buying her new pairs. But the one about needing money to put food on the table didn't fare too well, not surprisingly, since cupcakes are actual food and there I was holding a whole tray. In this particular case, though, I found the truth worked wonders.

"I'm selling cupcakes on account of my mom won't steal me a trampoline," I'd say, and I sold panloads. At ten cents apiece, though, I never did make enough to buy myself a major piece of playground equipment, so I didn't get the trampoline. Instead I just amassed big pile of dimes, which I decided was better than a trampoline. I liked how a mess of dimes felt against my palms, all small, slippery, and flat. I took them out of their metal bank every day and played with them, letting them slip through my fingers, laughing like a mad little miser. "Mine, mine, all mine!" I'd cackle.

Then the pile mysteriously started diminishing. At first it was just one or two dimes at a time—an amount someone wrongly thought I wouldn't miss. Then one morning my pile was downright paltry! My father was home that morning because he just lost his job selling trailers again, and I'd overheard my mother being really upset because she personally decorated some of the trailers at the big trade show, and she was lamenting the loss of two carved mallard ducks and other accessories she'd paid for and wanted back. But when my father left a job, he didn't go back, and those ducks were gone for good.

That morning, when my father gave my sisters and me our lunch money, he doled it out in dimes. I didn't say anything. Instead I just waited patiently, and eventually my pile of dimes began to grow again, as I knew it would. After that I took my pile to the swap meet every weekend until I found a carved duck. The lady wanted five dollars for it, and I thought about telling her one of my stories, but in the end opted on the truth and she let me have it for half my pile. The part she liked best, she said, was that I wanted to give it to my *father* to give to my mother. That and how I'd earned all those dimes my own goddam self.

I'S SERIOUSLY DIFFICULT not to cry all the time lately, and not just because I'm the cesspool of hormones everyone said I would become during the final stretch—and I mean *stretch*—of this whole experiment in spawning I've been these past few months. For one thing, I cry because I wonder, Jesus God!, am I *always* going to be this waddling, puffy-faced planet with swollen feet who can't even pick things up? Don't get me wrong, I was never a good housekeeper. I take after my own mother, who was so oblivious to the roaches in our house that she didn't notice we had a problem until they started attacking our heads while we were in bed.

So I consider it a huge accomplishment over my upbringing that I specialize in picking things up. I'm not good at *cleaning*, per se, because I understand that cleaning entails the use of, like, sponges and special gloves and stuff. I seriously don't get that. I can stare at my bathtub for an entire morning wondering why the hell it doesn't clean itself since I splash water on it every day when I shower, but when I see a bath towel on the floor, I'm really good at picking it up and hanging it on the doorknob. See, that's what I do, I *pick things up*. Now—huge, bloaty bag of bacon fat that I am—I can't even do that. If I drop something I have to kick it all the way to Lary's place so he can pick it up. Sometimes he is not even home, and when he gets home he has to yell, "Why the hell is there a *spatula* on my floor?" Then I have to cry.

I cry all the time. And if I ever stop to wonder what the hell it is I'm crying about, I cry even harder because, oh, my God!, I'm gonna have a baby. You would be amazed at how pregnant a woman can get before that fact really sinks in. Here I am, knocked up now for eight and a half months, and the whole inevitability that all this will culminate in a squiggly little ball of bone and flesh with *eyeballs* and everything didn't really hit me until I attended the perinatal classes at Crawford Long Hospital last weekend.

It was there that they showed us those *movies*. Those grainy, gory, homegrown *snuff films*, with the difference being that, instead of someone ending up dead at the conclusion, someone ends up the opposite of that ("It's alive! Alive!"), a twist that is almost as horrifying if you ask me. Inevitably there is a point in these films in which the mother becomes a growling, eye-rolling, foaming-at-the-mouth demon who can do little but thrash her head from side to side. At this point she puts her legs up and all of a sudden out pops this *other head*! It stays that way for awhile—I swear I think the obstetrician slows things down on purpose at this point so everyone can take in the "wonder" of it all—and the mother is lying there swinging her head around in silent agony while *the other head* is blinking its eyeballs. It was the Attack of the Two-Headed Creature!

All of a sudden it occurred to me that, Jesus God!, this is what I have to go through to get to the other side, the side with the little knit booties and the baby jumper with "Born to Suck Tittie" embroidered across the front that a lesbian couple contributed to my baby shower. *I have to become the two-headed creature!* So, needless to say, I was still crying in my seat when the lights went up and the other future mothers had left the room for a snack break.

"Hey, you're gonna do fine. Everything will be fine," Daniel tried to console me.

"That's just not *natural!*" I sobbed into the cell phone.

"C'mon," he said, "you need to be stronger. You need to pick yourself up." At that I stopped gibbering. I can do that, I thought. Picking things up is my specialty.

DON'T FIND IT FUNNY that the delivery-room nurses decided to nickname my baby "Tomato Face." I mean, aren't most babies born with big red heads? And another thing, nobody told me there was so much seepage involved in new motherhood. I feel like a faulty Tupperware container. Actually Lary did try to warn me, but who can take him seriously? Especially when it comes to motherhood. He reminded me I shouldn't bring my big-headed baby to his place because she would die—not that he would kill her himself, but that his place, a former abandoned candy factory, is about as safe for children as a bag of broken glass thrown at a spinning lawnmower blade, what with all the industrial tools Lary leaves strewn about. I don't know what he uses that equipment for, but I think he might have sawed a car in half once. That's probably what those pieces are under a tarp in the alleyway behind his warehouse. Anyway, with all those tools I don't see why he can't build my baby a protective iron bubble so I can hang out at his place like I used to. I don't think that's asking too much.

Because otherwise I'm pretty much a prisoner here in my own home, a walking lactating lunch bucket for my newborn. What's worse is that it looks like I'll have to give up my God hobby as well. Back when Grant decided to become a fugitive from mediocrity and gave away everything he owned, I was happy to get his collection of crudely painted roadside religious signs. They're propped up against the outside of my house right now, blaring "Get Right with God," "Hell Hurts," and "Repent Immediately!" The problem is people in my neighborhood think I mean it, and they're mistaking me for some kind of missionary, and lately all the roadside flotsam who beg for money at intersections have been knocking at my door. "I am not a nun!" I have to shriek. "I am a recovering slut!"

Sadder still is that the panhandlers are pretty much my only daytime company, captive in my home like I am, which is ironic because I didn't buy this place to hang out in it. It's only six minutes away from Poncey Highlands where I used to live, so I figured I'd always be over in my old neighborhood drinking lattes and tequila shooters and whatnot, and maybe I'd sleep in my house on those rare nights I didn't stay out having wild sex with traveling Irish rugby players. In the meantime this place would quietly increase in value until I sold it for an assload of money and retired to a small island off the coast of Cancun like Grant did, only for real. There I would bake under the sun until my skin turned to beef jerky. It was a good plan.

But things never go according to plan. In fact, I think if you're really attached to controlling your future, you should plan for the opposite of what you want just to confuse the cosmic comedians whose sole job is to figure out what you think your future should hold so they can preclude it from ever happening. Because never, after a decade of making do with the faded memories of most of the members of my original family, did I think that I'd eventually grow a new one of my own. Never did I plan for this little sprogette, whose name is Milly, and whose head is still big but not red anymore.

KNOCKERS ARE NEW TO ME. I bought my first bra when I was twenty-eight years old, and even then it was just an accessory. When I backpacked across the Greek islands six years earlier, I went topless as often as a toddler and was hardly more endowed. After returning to school that same year, I wore T-shirts with the sleeve holes ripped down to the waist, affording occasional side peeks at my tiny tits, and causing the head of the Bible club to complain.

So I was never burdened with the desire for boobs. I once saw a girl on the patio at the Local who had fake breasts big enough to be seen with the naked eye from outer space, yet she wore a T-shirt with "STOP STARING AT THESE" written across her chest. If I were king, I would make her wear a sign that says, "I Paid Good Money to Become a Physical Freak, Ogle All You Want." I think it would also be fitting for to cap her nipples with little rotating propellers that beep warnings like an approaching forklift, because a rack like hers is a hazard. I wonder how many of her ex-boyfriends are wearing eye patches.

So, you know, I never understood the appeal of big boobs, and then I acquired them, and now it's *really* a mystery to me. Three days after I spawned, I awoke in the hospital and found that two fleshy foreign objects had landed on my chest. They were so big that I couldn't lay on my side because they'd bang together like boulders, which caused precisely enough pain to make my skeleton rip from my flesh and cling to the ceiling until an orderly came by with a broom and swatted it down. Occasionally, a nurse would stop in and latch my baby onto me like a little vampire, and then I'd think, "Oh, my God, I'm a damn dairy cow!"

So I figured these breasts would just go away some

day, overnight maybe, like the way they came. But to this day they are, literally, still hanging around. Not too long ago, I made the mistake of working an overnight trip figuring if they got engorged, I could just hang them over of the side of the hotel bed or something so they could drain. What a mistake that was. At optimum production cycle and no baby within reach to trip the release valve, my breasts exploded like loaded cigars. Or at least that's what it felt like, because they grew big enough to be anchored by Boy Scouts in the Thanksgiving Day Parade. I thought I had some kind of flesh-eating breast cancer. On the plane home, I pilfered all the free sanitary napkins in the lavatory, shoved them into my bra and squeezed. I guess I was thinking that if I could just juice my boobs like oranges, all would be well.

All was not well. My breasts were hard as hunks of Formica, and from the waist up I looked like a cheap stripper who had gotten her boob job done by some guy in a garage. All I could do was stumble off the plane and race back to Milly, who had been lovingly cared for in my absence. Maybe I'm imagining this part, because she's only six months old after all, but I could swear you can tell by her face the kind of sight I was, limping toward her with snarly hair, fevered brow, broken buttons, and Kotex on my tits.

The next day I decided it was time to properly start closing down this lactating lunch counter, and Milly took to the bottle for good. I had been her personal feedbag for months, so I thought I'd relish this moment. But instead, watching her eat without me, I felt a sudden pain in my chest. It was an ache, really, an ache to the beat of words spoken to me by a kindly old doorman at Waffle House a month earlier. He stood smiling over Milly's carrier, her tiny hand grasping his wizened finger, and suddenly his eyes rounded knowingly. "One day you'll blink," he said, "and she'll be grown."

LARY WON'T LET ME BORROW his Jesus Christ costume this year, and I don't see why he's so attached to it. It's just a bed sheet, after all, with the words, "I'm Jesus Christ, Your Fucking Saviour," scrawled across the back in black marker.

"Goddammit, you walking stain on the butt end of the earth," I shriek, because sometimes shrieking works with Lary, "Gimme it."

"Sorry," he says, "why don't you just make your own?"

Of course I could make my own costume, but I get too complicated. I can't just be a hobo or a serial killer or something simple. No. I have to be, like, an *octopus* with battery operated, individually animated tentacles with real suction cups and stuff.

One year I was a sorceress, laden with a cauldron, even, inside of which was an operating *fog machine*. My actual costume consisted of so much black lace, black chiffon, bejeweled brooches, and mystically glowing crystals that I looked like a walking gothic mansion. I was so exhausted after putting it all on that I paused to catch my breath and awakened four hours later, sitting upright on my couch with the illuminated skull atop my staff still blinking feebly.

I can't do that this year. I can't. Already I have six pumpkins. Six. Yesterday I almost bought six more, but I had to stop myself because I was at one of those specialty markets that only offer organic, kosher, kinetic whatever-the-fuck farmed vegetables, and six pumpkins cost more than my entire car payment. So I put them all back, promising myself that, first chance, I'm stopping at one of those crap-ass grocery stores that sell pumpkins the size of Cinderella's carriage, only all mutated. Those cost about a buck apiece because they've been injected with polypropylene and cultivated inside giant microwaves, probably.

So I can't possibly get started on a costume. It just might kill me. I need something simple. But since Lary won't loan me his Jesus Christ costume I'll have to battle my bent toward complicating things. Maybe I can just wear one of those stupid headbands with bloody eyeballs on springs, but I'm afraid the line has been crossed and it's impossible to turn back.

I'm reminded of one of my theology teachers in college—World Religion was the course—who told us on the first day of class to "leave now if you don't want to complicate your life." I didn't know what the hell she meant. It's just *knowledge*, I thought, but when none of us took her up on leaving right then, the professor shook her head and said, "There'll be no turning back."

Until then I'd basically put as much thought into religion as my aborted Sunday school dabblings allowed me to have. I believed in heaven and hell. I believed Jesus looked like a honey-haired underwear model. I believed in the basic paper-doll parade of characters the Bible put forth.

My mother said we were welcome to our own convictions as long as they weren't made under duress, which explains why she'd yanked us out of Sunday school. Our preacher had me under major duress, having told me I'd go to hell for not tithing properly.

"That's just goddam ignorance," my mother said.

But ignorance is the natural state for budding college students, and I'd retained that arrested image of religion until the day when my professor said there was no turning back. I swear I think I was happy until then, happy in my ignorance and the simpleness of my life. But sometimes there is a difference between a happy life and a meaningful life.

My professor, surprisingly, proceeded to teach us tolerance, which is an astonishingly painful lesson. I swear, it's agony. The pain comes from revisiting all your past apathies through the eyes of those you injured. Like the time I helped humiliate a Hindu girl in fifth grade. *Fifth grade.* She was fragile and beautiful and raven-haired and for some reason she'd fainted in the bathroom near the playground at school.

We thought she was faking it, so it was my idea to test her by plucking the jewel out of her nose. Only back then those things didn't exactly pluck, they kinda screwed in, and we weren't all that delicate. In short, we practically ripped her a new nostril, and she woke up screaming, and she kept screaming when she noticed her jewel missing. God, that girl could scream.

No one knows what happened to the jewel, but after that the Indian girl never, ever spoke another word to us again. Not one, not even when we tried to get her to scream again, which was often. Unfortunately, nothing is more unbearable to an adolescent than a dignified quiet. I ache to go back there all the time in my mind, to the beautiful little screaming Hindu girl. I want to look into her injured eyes and implore, "Say something." I want to apologize for making her tolerate my ignorance. I want it to be that simple, but nothing is simple anymore. Everything is complicated, and there is no turning back.

BILL HAD A HEART ATTACK in Nicaragua, of all the inconsiderate places to almost croak. He's been half dead for about a century now, and it would have been *so simple* for him to keel over in any number of *accessible* places, like Las Vegas, for chrissakes. He spent three weeks there recently, trying to hide from my sister Cheryl, who lives there and found him anyway. He avoided her, I'm thinking, because he gambled the money she gave him to start over after the bar he opened in Costa Rica sucked every cent out of his life. Bill likes to put all his chips on the table, so whether he wins or loses the results are big.

Good thing he won in Vegas. In Costa Rica Bill hadn't been so lucky. He'd been blathering about that place almost from the day my mother introduced him to me, about how he was going to open a bar on the beach there, with caramel-colored Ticas feeding him peyote pellets between tandem-action tongue baths or whatever. That was almost fifteen years ago, and he was living in his car, so I didn't take him too seriously.

But whaddo I know? It turns out by that time he had made and lost four fortunes, and years later he would amass his fifth, but first he became my mother's best friend. When they'd met at that auction in Chula Vista, they were both bidding on a box of mostly broken ceramic beagles with bobbing heads, which I think is appropriate. Like I said, if there were ever two broken toys in the world—two total misfits searching for a haven in the storm of conformity—it was my mother and her friend Bill. At the time she had just lost her job designing defense missiles because government bombs had fallen out of fashion, and he was a paranoid, foul-mouthed, chain-smoking, misanthropic, morally ambiguous old tarpit of an entrepreneur about to get rich again selling junk.

Yes, junk. They became junk dealers, my mother and Bill, with a warehouse six times the size of my house by the time my mother fell ill. He was with me at her bedside when she died, and I just now realized for the first time that I've known Bill longer than my mother ever did, not that he's been bearable all this time.

But at least he made it to Costa Rica. In the mid-nineties he sold all his businesses, headed to the beach town of Quepos, and bought the biggest bar there. The bar turned out to be much nicer than I expected, with sixty or so festively painted tables on a point of turf overlooking the ocean. Earlier I'd gotten e-mails from other Atlanta residents who'd made it there before me, telling me they'd met my "stepfather" and heard the whole story about how I'd once won a bar fight in Ensenada by choking an assailant with her own necklace. I never corrected them on the stepfather issue, though for all I know Bill isn't above having secretly married my mother. I mean, he certainly wasn't above secretly using my social security number to open a bank account once.

But like I said, Bill puts all his chips on the table, and in Costa Rica he lost everything. Then, after his casino caper that increased the money my sister gave him tenfold, he moved to Nicaragua and opened what amounts to be, I guess, a small hotel/brothel. He's been raving about the idea since his experience in Costa Rica, where he noted that almost every hotel is also a whorehouse. From what I understand, Bill had quite a cash register humming at his new place until this heart attack hit him. Cheryl plans to go to him, and has sent me a card with directions to get there. "Take a taxi from the Managua airport to Granada," it read, "and don't wear any jewelry."

I'd already turned her down once, over the phone when she called to tell me Bill's condition. "I can't traipse off to Nica—goddam—*RAGUA*," I protested. "Don't they kidnap Americans there?"

"Only important Americans," she qualified. "Look, Holly, it's *Bill*," she implored.

It's Bill, that crusty bucket of phlegm. That big-eyed, big-mouthed, big-hearted old acid vat who held my mother's hand as she died in my arms. I wouldn't have thought him capable of crying if I hadn't seen it with my own eyes, but there he was that day, holding her hand and then me.

It's Bill. Bill, who has the personality of a honey-covered warthog but nonetheless taught me that it matters, you know, how you handle things, like the slipping away of precious people you can't keep clutched to you forever. Now he's hurt and, God, I really hope it's true about the Nicaraguan kidnappers, how they're only interested in important people and not us, the lost and flailing, the little broken toys of the world whose only importance is to each other.

I **WAS ABSOLUTELY UNPREPARED** for the house fire, which is sadly on par with my preparation for all things in general. For example, I still have a can of yams as big as a bongo drum left over from the impending holocaust the Y2K crossover was supposed to be, a reminder it was not me who had the foresight to stockpile food. No, Daniel is the one with the foresight. He brought the can of yams and hid it on the bottom shelf of my baker's rack behind the recycle bin. Why he felt he had to hide the yams, I don't know. Maybe he figured that, at the strike of midnight, marauding Y2K-unprepared people would storm my house and, seeing that we were unprepared as well, simply take their torches and move onto the next house, after which Daniel could pull out his can of yams and exclaim, "Ha! Fooled them!" and then we would feast until the world was right again. But having friends with the foresight to hide yams is pretty much the extent of my ability to prepare for the future.

Honnie and Todd are having to prepare for the future as well, and they have put their plans for parenthood on hold, seeing as how they can't fathom raising a baby in a home across the street from a crack house and next door to a violent drug dealer. It really, seriously, doesn't help *at all* that the drug dealer next door has taken to setting their house on fire.

"Great values," Honnie says dryly. She is always very dry, whereas if I were her I wouldn't be dry at all. I'd be bawling my eyes out. The fire was set in the basement and was extinguished by the fire department before it spread past the kitchen. The smoke damage alone set them back basically to the point they were at when they bought the place, before they'd spent months renovating the interior.

The police are absolutely no help. In fact they are the opposite of help. This is Atlanta's notorious Zone C, after all, made famous for corruption within the force. The officers are probably paid so much by the dealers not to do their job that they're quite irked when people like Honnie and her family, and me, move here and expect a fundamental showing of effort. The reason, I figure, is because it interferes with their bribe taking and prostitute killing.

I feel sorry for the poor prostitutes, too. Not only do they have to fuck the skank-ass flotsam who are their normal clientele, but they have to bow to extorted blowjobs demanded by the police officers, too. You gotta marvel at the power of crack cocaine, you really do. I cannot think of a harder job than being a whore, and for something to have such a hold on you, to the point where you sacrifice everything to it, to the point you have nothing left to offer except your own orifices again and again, that is a mighty hook to have in you, I swear.

But still I guess it gets to them once in a while, these whores in our neighborhood. Rumor has it they resist occasionally, sometimes to their extreme detriment. Two have been shot recently by police. One of them was Pox Face, who is dead now. The other shot whore is not dead, or not as dead as Pox Face, anyway. The police said they did it in self-defense, because each girl had suddenly wielded a knife or pepper spray or both, though it's reported that Pox Face had been shot in the back. Her sister hangs out on Dill Avenue up the street from my house, and she herself is a prostitute, and she complains all the time about having to submit to the sexual whims of the police, and how it will be even worse now that she knows they killed her sister, who was nonviolent and didn't even own shoes let alone a canister of pepper spray.

So I figure the police are too busy wagging their dicks at these girls to do anything productive. I thank God every day for my dog Cookie, a pit bull that looks like a furry cross between a crocodile and a barracuda. She has teeth as big as ballpoint pens, though she's never bitten a soul except me when she was a puppy. These drug dealers don't know that, though, and they cut a wide path when they see me coming their way with her on a leash. I had no idea a mean-looking dog would be so effective in warding off evil in a bad neighborhood, but I'm convinced it's the one thing that separates my house from Honnie and Todd's. I figure if they had a mean-looking dog, as opposed to the sweet-looking little boxer puppy they presently have, then maybe the drug dealer would not be so emboldened as to set their house on fire.

But who's to say why they are targeted and I am not, and who's to say I won't be next? So I am trying to prepare for that. I put in an alarm system and I make sure Cookie keeps looking mean, even though if anyone broke into my house to set it on fire she'd probably foil them only because she peed on their efforts out of sheer excitement to see them. But the drug dealers next door don't need to know that. They can just keep on believing she'll rip their heads right off their shoulders. It's a small comfort, but it's all I have to rely on right now.

YOU'D THINK HE'D BE MORE INVENTIVE, because Lary is nothing if not glorious about meting out humiliation, but he probably went easy on Milly because she's a baby, and a beautiful one at that. So all he came up with was the stamping of her head.

"You should put 'REJECT' in red letters, right on her forehead," he suggests. "I really do have a stamp for that, you know."

"She is not a *reject*, you bag of crap!" I shrieked, but my heart wasn't in the shrieking, and Lary could tell. God, this has got me in a slough of despondency, this whole thing with Milly's preschool—or her lack of a preschool, to be more accurate. I'd gotten the phone message the night before. "I'm sorry to say Milly didn't get in," said the administrator, "but the good news is that everyone else did."

Everyone—*everyone*—but Milly. I'm told they had exactly one excess applicant and Milly lost the lottery. "Look at her," Lary says, "she has no idea she's starting life out as a loser."

Christ, how's *that* for hitting a chord? And he's right, she has no idea. She seems perfectly happy hanging out with me all day. But shouldn't she be *out there*, interacting with the world and other babies? I mean besides Lary, who only qualifies as an infant in the emotional sense. He's offered to babysit before, but only because he's completely confident I'd let a rabid raccoon babysit my daughter before resorting to him. I mean, last week he let her play with a big rusty razor blade, for chrissakes! Or at least that's what it looked like.

"It's a spatula," Lary said, "calm down." We were at his place preparing for the cocktail party he throws every other year to remind himself there's a world outside his warehouse—because he really can close himself up alone in there for months at a time sometimes—and he'd had enough of me and my multitude of minor freaks over Milly's safety.

"She's not going to kill herself with a kitchen utensil," he said, pointing to Milly's prone body strapped in her stroller. "Look at her, she's safe."

Look at her. She's not safe. This is Lary's place we're talking about; roll her two feet in any direction and she'll end up with fish hooks in her head. But how is this any less perilous than the world in general? Even Lary locks himself away from it occasionally, preferring his own personal den of hidden disasters to the uncertainty of *out there.*

Safety, ha! I thought, here's to hoping there is such a thing. I have a coconut shell carved in the shape of a monkey's face I've kept for decades because it reminds me of the year I lived in Melbourne Beach, Florida. I was nine and never wore shoes that year. I simply leapt out of the house shoeless every day and walked to the river where I'd catch sailor fish from the pier and let them go. On blustery days I climbed to the crests of pine trees and let the wind sway me back and forth. I wish I had other items to remind me of this period in my life, the last time I felt completely safe, because . . . well, let's just say you would not catch me shoeless today. Today I cover my toes, among other things.

And I shield Milly, but I want her to be spiritually barefoot, too. I want her to spring up each day unweighted by the bunk that will eventually mire us all in time. Mired like me. Like I feel *so bad* about the preschool.

"Get used to it," says Lary, who has taken to calling Milly "The Unchosen One." He reminds me of the regrettable period a few years ago in which he, Grant, and I once sought self-improvement from professional motivators. Lary even went as far as to join a seminar with the aim to make him a more loving person. After the second session they asked him not to return. And Grant! Grant didn't even get that far; they barred his attendance after one phone call. Me? I was told "there's nothing we can do to help you." We gathered at Daniel's place afterward and laughed about it, completely certain we were safe from ever fitting in.

"So you see? Milly is safe," Lary tries to console. "Safe from ever being normal."

DAMN, **THEY DID NOT** find the body to match the severed head in a sack after all. I tell you, I was wary right from the beginning, when Michael called to tell me he'd heard on the news they'd finally found the decapitated corpse to match the head in a plastic bag police found five years ago in my neighborhood, Capitol View. For one, that particular headless torso would just be bones by now, wouldn't it? It sounded like the one they found in Walker County last fall was *fresher* than that. So unless the killer was keeping it frozen all these years that scenario did not make sense.

I was right. It turned out the Walker County corpse had its own head, in Johnson City, Tennessee, with three holes in it. Not only *that*, they think the killer is the same guy who cut off the heads and hands of a seventeen-year-old newlywed last October. That boy's head and hands were found floating in a lake out-side Johnson City, and later the rest of his body, plus that of his teenage wife, were found in a self-storage bin in the same vicinity, relatively. The suspected killer is in jail in New York on "unrelated drug charges," but, person-ally, if you ask me, I think drugs are definitely related to this, including the still-unidentified head and sacks of other body parts they found scattered in Capitol View years ago. Until they find the killer or the identities of the people who lost their parts, it all seems so unfinished to me. It all just seems to be hanging there, like a safe sus-pended by dental floss, waiting to drop. And I *hate* that.

I would prefer things not to be scattered. I would pre-fer that they find all the pieces and match them up in little labeled forensic tubs and notify family members and other interested parties (like me) that these pieces, though still dismembered, are at least no longer disembodied. If it were my murdered limbs, my dead ass would feel lousy knowing that parts of my corpse were still out there, waiting to be stumbled upon by neighborhood kids. My stand is that your own cut-up body parts are personal, and you don't want just anybody looking at them. That is my biggest peeve about plane crashes, too, because I seriously loathe the idea of my body chunks showering down on complete strangers.

But I guess there are certain things to which you just have to become accustomed. Sometimes things remain scattered. They stay unfinished. The pieces stay missing. In fact they almost always do. Like I made my father a coat once, all except for the sleeve cuffs, because I could not figure out how the hell to attach them. I got past everything else—and this was a complicated coat, mind you, with duck down insulation and zippers and snaps and stuff— and I mastered them all except for the sleeves. So for two years that coat stayed unfinished, a masterpiece of intricate handiwork defeated by simple sleeve cuffs, which remained missing pieces.

My father kept expecting it, though. I'd been making coats since I was fifteen, the year before my mother left him. Call it a phase, but I used to like making complicated things from scratch. There were hundreds of pieces that had to come together for these coats, and I would personally burn the edges of each article of insulation by candle to keep the nylon frays from scattering, because who likes to leave things scattered? But for my dad's coat I decided to graduate to knit sleeve cuffs, and that is what conquered me.

Finally I just hemmed the sleeves without the cuffs, which was kind of crazy because who wants a down jacket with no sleeve cuffs to keep the snow out? Even though we lived in California, I still envisioned my father having to change a flat in a blizzard somewhere, grateful that he had his daughter's handmade down jacket to stave off the storm, only now his wrists would be frostbitten because important pieces were missing. But I finished it as best I could, because my father kept expecting it, and about four months after I finally gave it to him he died, which was not expected at all.

My sister and mother went to collect his effects, and upon their return they gave the coat back to me. My mother said the coat was not hanging in his closet with his other clothes, but rather from a nail on the wall in his dining room. "He must have liked looking at it," she said. So I took the jacket back and hung it from a nail on the wall in my room. I liked looking at it, too. I no longer thought of it as unfinished, as having scattered or missing pieces. When I looked at it the only piece missing was the man inside.

M**Y FRIEND DENNIS** is visiting from San Francisco, and I'm all atwitter. He's one of my oldest friends, and I seriously love this person. He has saved me from so much. In fact, the next to the last time I saw him he was saving me from a cluster fuck, and I mean that literally.

I was in San Francisco, not to visit Dennis but my other friend Joanie, who had a guy she wanted me to meet, seeing as how my then-boyfriend had just dumped me like a load of toxic waste—I mean he *ugly* dumped me. I came home one day and there were lists taped up all over our dining room walls, titled "Five-Year Goals," "Ten-Year Goals," and so on. I had to go and ask where I fit on his lists. I seriously think I could have kept that truth at bay for awhile, probably for goddam decades, but I guess it wasn't in me, that capacity for falsehood. I had to go and ask him, and he had to go and tell me.

So that Thanksgiving, I mean that very weekend, he moved me out of our apartment. I like to think it wouldn't have been so hard if he hadn't been so happy throughout, but the truth is it would have been hard nonetheless. It made for a bad Thanksgiving, me alone eating mushroom gravy out of the can and watching Dennis Miller's talk show back before they stupidly pulled it from network television. But hell, at least I had the odd comfort of my ex-boyfriend, who would call occasionally to say he'd forgiven himself for how he'd treated me.

During this time Joanie lost all her worldly possessions in a wildfire, and was living in a furnished apartment outside San Francisco until she could recoup. I went there thinking I could help her cope, because I think it's times like this that your friends serve as emotional oxygen to your breathless heart, and you must pass from one to the other, borrowing air until you can breathe on your own again. But once I arrived, Joanie didn't turn to me for comfort.

No. She took comfort in a most odd way. First, that man she wanted me to meet? It was her boyfriend's best friend, but by the time I'd arrived, she'd developed a crush on him herself. "Joanie, whichever one you decide you want, I'll distract the other, okay?" I told her, not fathoming she'd decide not to decide and end up in bed with both.

I swear, it's not easy pretending you're asleep on the couch when three people are fucking on the floor right beside you. By morning they'd mercifully moved to the bedroom and, left to wander her apartment on my own, I tried to drown out the howlings coming from Joanie's bedroom by making long-distance calls on her phone.

"Just join in," Lary suggested. "That's what I'd do."

"Retard," I said, "I would rather rip out my kidneys with a crowbar."

But Lary could only comfort me for so long before he had to go grade a door down with an industrial sander or something, so soon I was alone again, and utterly miserable. Seriously, there's nothing sadder—nothing that'll make you more certain you're wasting your life—than spending the day in a strange apartment in a strange city waiting for your friend to finish getting fucked by strange men.

Eventually I ran out of numbers to call and chose, simply, to leave quietly, and for good. Joanie's apartment was serviced by an exterior security gate, and once past that there was no turning back. Plus, my coat was locked in her car, and I had to abandon it to walk, freezing, to the car-parts store on the corner.

It was there I called Dennis. It had been three years since I'd last seen him, in San Diego where he served as a college intern at the magazine where I worked as a tortured copy editor, but still he pulled up to the curb fifteen minutes later, where I was waiting by the phone booth clutching a plastic sack.

"What's in the bag?" he asked.

"A headlight," I said. He didn't even ask why I bought a headlight in California when my car was in Georgia.

He took me to a coffeehouse, and there I poured forth, not just about Joanie, but about everything. "You'd think the man you loved would include you in his five-year plan, or even his ten-year plan," I blubbered, recounting my most recent Eiffel-Tower-in-the-ass moment. I'd been having them a lot lately, doleful reminders that the world was not my personal balloon on a string after all. "You'd think I'd fucking *fit* somewhere."

Dennis just let me leak until I didn't have any air left, then he took me to his family home to sleep in his sister's bedroom. What I remember most about his childhood home is the counter spaces. They were cluttered with wondrous things it must have taken decades to collect, and I loved the way his house smelled, like heavily peppered vegetables.

I don't know how Dennis explained to his family why his college friend showed up coatless on a cold winter day to spend the night, but I think it says a lot for them that they let me stay as long as I wanted, sitting there at their dining table, taking an odd comfort in the commingling of aromas that made up their family. They let me borrow their air until I could breathe on my own again, and for that I will always be grateful.

'M NOT ALL THAT PROUD that one of my first words in Italian is "maggot." You'd think I'd come up with something a little more useful, like "help," but I've been here with Milly for two weeks and I still don't know that word.

I'm here on a company-paid excursion to learn this language and put another interpreter qualification under my belt, which will take me far in the eyes of the nearly bankrupt airline I barely still work for. I qualified as an interpreter years ago in German and Spanish, but now all of a sudden I've become rusty at picking up languages. My problem is I keep searching through the dictionary for basic words of immediate use, like "need" or "have," and I get all caught up with phrases I see on the way, like "acid test." I see that and I suddenly think I cannot possibly communicate with Italians without knowing how to say "acid test," it's such a useful phrase! Or "zombie" or "polyunsaturated." Seriously, these words are so universal, and I want to make it a point to learn words that matter.

For example, I remember years ago when my older sister's Argentine ex-boyfriend, a busboy who could barely speak English, once used the word "compensation" in a sentence. It can be an impressive word when it's the only decipherable one in a slew of words being spewed forth by an angry Argentine demanding restitution for having slipped in the alleyway behind his apartment building. It was a good performance, too, seeing as how he himself had unscrewed the bulb in the building's exterior lamp to ensure there'd be insufficient lighting when he ventured back there.

Yes, this man bypassed all the lesser words of the English language and cut right to the one everyone respects. I hear he owns a car dealership now.

So I always figured that would be a good way to absorb other languages; just pick the words that scare people and say them over and over until you own a car dealership or something. But I think you have to be a certain kind of person to recognize those words readily—not a person like me. For example, I'm not satisfied with knowing how to say a simple "thank you" in another language. I want to know how to say it in the most officious way possible. I want to know how to say, "I'm delighted by your kindness," or "Your generosity amazes me," or "I am humbled by the bounteousness of your humanity."

People are generally flattered by my method, but I don't see any of them clamoring to give me car dealerships. Even so, I like being able to thank people in pretty ways. Sometimes I don't even say it to anyone in particular. I just say the words because I like the way they sound.

My mother always told me I spoke my very first word when I was a few months shy of two years old, and that word was "cigarette." In actuality, though, the word was just "get," but since I was indicating my mother's cigarette with my hand when I said it, she thought it obvious I wanted to try a hit. "Whaddaya know? A kid after my own heart," she said proudly; then she sat me atop the ironing board and put her lit Salem menthol in my mouth.

I coughed so violently I can actually recall the incident—it's flapping around in my head like an escapee from the compendium of memories that are supposed to be locked in the subconscious of your first years, along with what it felt like to be born and whatnot. I remember sitting there on the ironing board, hacking my lungs out like a veteran, while my mother patted me on the back as if a good burping was all I needed to get me breathing again.

My father interrupted his own puffing to castigate her for a minute, telling her she shouldn't share her cigarette with a two-year-old, taking care to part his own cloak of secondhand smoke so she could see he was serious. "She's gotta know if she likes it," my mother said, "the earlier the better."

By the time I was thirteen I had a pack-a-day habit. Then suddenly that same year I'd decided I'd had enough and simply quit. Looking back, I guess thirteen qualifies as an early age to determine if you like smoking or not. If my mother were here I'd thank her very officiously for getting the wheels rolling so soon in that regard. I would say something in Italian perhaps, something like, "Your compassion is a vast ocean among mere puddles."

But I can't, those chances are past. Now I have Milly, and her first words emerged not long ago, like a foggy picture finally come into focus. Weeks beforehand, those words just sounded like the cooing of a pigeon. "Hoo koo. Hoo koo," Milly would trill, always while handing you something. Then the sound evolved, "Hank hoo," until one day it came out clear as a bell. "Thank you," she said as she handed me the torn label from a can of cat food.

At her words—her first words—my heart almost clawed its way out of my chest, so desperate it was to attach itself to her like lovesick putty. I held her for five hundred years after that, or at least I wish I could have. "Thank you," she kept repeating. "Thank you. Thank you." Whaddaya know? I thought, soaking the top of her head with my tears. A kid after my own heart.

DURING MY FIRST freshman year of college I was the same as most of my fellow students—drug-addled and ignorant as a child. I even used to be jealous of my truly drug-addicted friends for being so skinny. "Damn," I'd think, "look at that bitch, she has to jump around in the shower just to get wet! I *hate* her."

I myself tried very hard to be an addict during that year. I was seventeen and living in a bay-front apartment with two other totally self-involved slags, who, when they weren't fucking my boyfriend behind my back, were introducing him to a harem of other girls for basic blow-job consideration.

I tell you, that's the problem with dating hot guys. This one wasn't just hot, but drop-jaw hot, with long blond hair and eyes as blue as blowtorch flames. He looked like an angel, but *evil*. God, he was evil.

"Do you love me?" he once asked despondently. I wondered if that might be the reason he was acting so strange lately. Oh, the poor, handsome, sad little god. "Yeah," I replied tentatively.

"That's the problem," he said, exasperated, "I don't love you."

Evil, I tell you. By the way, that is the only time I ever punched a man.

But he stayed in my life for as long as I let him. He once tried to pimp me off on a friend, and another time he and another drunk friend tried to gang rape me while my roommates laughed in the living room, ignoring my cries. Finally our brassy hairdresser neighbor heard me screaming from the sidewalk and simply walked in through our open front door. "What the hell's going on here?" she shouted. At that the guys let me go and continued their marathon coke-snorting session in my kitchen.

I tried to let all this be okay with me. I tried to not care when I'd come home after my third work shift for the day to find the son of the owner of the Mexican restaurant where my roommates worked waiting for me in my bed like he was entitled to be there.

"Who is that asshole in my bed?" I'd ask the crowd of other strangers in my place. They rolled their eyes in a universal signal of indifference.

I was on my way to fitting in, I think, when thank God my old friend Kathy came to visit. She'd driven the two hours south from Torrance to San Diego, where I had moved since the two of us attended high school together, to assess my living situation.

"Look at the bay!" I'd say excitedly. "It's right outside our window!"

She was unimpressed. She could care less about the close proximity of the ocean if it meant sharing an apartment with "these bitchy pigs," indicating my roommates, who at the time were in the other room passed out under a pile of guys. "Get yer shit," she said. "We're outta here." She began to gather my things.

And that is how I didn't become a drug addict my first freshman year in college. Kathy threw my possessions in the back of her impeccable '72 Ranchero, stopped for a minute to grab a pair of scissors and cut the crotches and armpits out of every single item of clothing my roommates had hanging on their clothesline over the carport, and moved my ass back up to Torrance, where I lived for the next four months with her sister Nadine in an apartment at least five miles from the beach.

Kathy herself lived with her mother in Rolling Hills, and she hadn't spoken to her father in years. The last time she saw him, she said, was when she caught sight of him early one morning asleep in his car parked outside a bar. His head was resting halfway outside his window, as was his arm, which dripped a trail of blood down the car door.

"Didn't you stop to help him?" I gasped.

"Fuck no," she said. "I hope the bastard died that day."

I used to wonder why Kathy would bother to save me but not her own father, but now I think I know the reason. It's because she must have tried. She must have tried so many times growing up to make herself matter more to him than his own addictions, and because she couldn't she probably took her father's failures personally, and hated him for making her hate herself.

I started my second freshman year in a different college the following fall, and four years later I got a call from Kathy. I'd stupidly lost touch with her since the fiasco of my first freshman year, and was surprised to hear her voice.

"I'm just walking out the door to graduate!" I yelled happily into the phone. Yes, I was about to graduate like a normal person, someone who wasn't hiding a secret first freshman year from school administrators. "Can I call you when I get back?" But I never talked to her again. I just hung up the phone like the person on the other line never saved my life at all, and, like an ignorant child, went about enjoying the gift she gave me without looking back.

MILLY'S MITTENS ARE MISSING. Yes, she wears mittens even though it's uncommonly hot out. They're tokens of comfort, I figure, like a blanket. Daniel calls them gloves and taught her to say it, only she often drops consonants when she talks. Our cats Lucy and Tinkerbell have become "Oosy" and "Inky" to Milly, and her gloves, which are so small they didn't even bother sewing fingers into them (they're just fuzzy pouchlike things) are "love." Yesterday, as I read the paper, I felt her fleeced little hand on my face, and I looked up to see her smiling at me, proudly sporting her mittens. "My love," she said sweetly.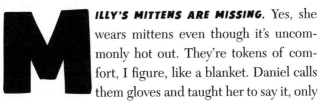

After that I knew I wouldn't be going to Nicaragua to help my sister Cheryl tend to my mother's best friend Bill, who, if he had any strength left, would probably use it to beat me with a fireplace poker. He's pissed at me for disclosing that the hotel he runs down there doubles as a brothel, which is no surprise. It was in Costa Rica (where he owned a bar that was as profitable as a huge hemorrhage inside his wallet) that he was about to go into business with a Nigerian woman who ran a hotel/whorehouse on the beach up the street. When I last visited he gave me a tour of the place, careful to point out the laundry facilities.

The arrangement was to have been that the African madam would populate Bill's bar with high-end whores every night, thus attracting an increase in patronage to his establishment. I don't know how Bill planned to compensate the madam, or perhaps he didn't, as they never did become business partners, though Bill left Costa Rica insisting his next business venture would be a facsimile of hers. I believed him, as Bill usually does what he says he will do.

Except die. He's been blathering about how his end is near for years, only he keeps breathing, regardless of his recent heart attack. My sister Cheryl is bereft, and dropped everything to be by his side. She loves Bill like a musty old bedtime toy treasured since her infancy. They've spent countless hours together since my mother's death; drinking, chain smoking, bitching about life in general and me in particular. I've changed, they complain. I used to be fun. I used to be brazen and braless, booze-addled, boy-crazy, and adventurous. Another one lost to the establishment, they toast, promising that they themselves will never sell out. And they never will.

Occasionally Bill tries to shake Cheryl free. It's nothing personal, it's just that Bill is unaccustomed to lasting attachments, even if you count my mother. When he met my mother she had only four years left to live, but through her Bill acquired Cheryl and, spiky old bag of magma that he is, Bill has become Cheryl's token of comfort in life. He can't shake her free. If he is lost she will find him, even in a jungle in Central America.

I made plans to go, too, and got Lary to commit as well. "We can fly into San Jose," I told him, "rent a car and drive seven hours over bad highways and unsettled political terrain until we get to Granada. Sound good?" It sounded *great* to Lary, who immediately started honing his duck-and-jab maneuvers in the event of an attempted kidnapping. In Central America, Lary and I would stand out like purple rhinos at a wedding reception. He has hair like a curly halo of albino tarantulas, and I myself have been loudly referred to as "bleachy-haired honky bitch," so by virtue of our un-Latin-ness alone we would make decent criminal targets.

"This'll be a great story to tell your grandkids," said Lary, who actually welcomed the prospect of living in a freshly dug dirt hole for a few months while demands for our ransom undoubtedly went ignored in Atlanta. "We'll escape by climbing a rope we made out of our own hair," he mused, excitedly. It started to sound fun even to me.

But then Milly's mittens went missing. I hovered helplessly as she toddled to every corner of our house. "My love! My love!" she sobbed with those big, uninhibited tears I sometimes wish I could still muster myself. It's difficult to describe the effect such a sight had on me, except to say that right then, for a second, I saw with clarity what was in store for me and my daughter. I realized we will lose each other one day, Milly and I, possibly more than once, but eventually for good. It's a reality as inescapable as it is unbearable to think about. She will long for me one day, and I will be out of her grasp, and she will have to make do with a token of comfort. What is life, after all, if not a succession of searches like this?

"You pussy," Lary chided when I bailed on our trip. I would have argued with him, but Milly was crying, and I was aching to help her find her lost love.

Snitches

THERE ARE TWO DRUG-ADDICT PANHANDLERS impersonating charity workers at the busy intersection near Honnie and Todd's house, and it's amazing anyone falls for their act. But I guess we are jaded in this neighborhood; we can spot a crack addict from five hundred paces, with their chalky lips, gray pallor, and taut cheekbones. But we are not newcomers, and there are a lot of newcomers coming through here lately.

They are coming for the same reason we first did, in search of an affordable home close to the city. But if they asked me, I'd tell them that, though the price of a home here is low, living here still comes at a very high cost.

Take the drug dealer next door to Honnie and Todd. He set their house on fire *again*. This was after they, along with other neighborhood activists, finally shut down the crack house across the street. After fruitless appeals to the police, they finally bypassed them and resorted to red tape to strangle the place. The county housing inspector slammed its owner with housing code violations like a blizzard of bureaucratic confetti, and rather than finance the mandated improvements, the owner simply emptied the house of tenants and put it up for sale. Now it's been transformed from a skanky, illegal boarding house to a piece of hot property.

"It's gorgeous in there," said the real-estate agent representing the house. "It's got four bedrooms, two bathrooms, and *four fireplaces*," and hardly any used condoms stuck to the porch anymore. But this agent knows that fact won't deter buyers, because at these prices most houses in Capitol View sell before the sign goes up in the yard, and this one was no exception. It sold in less than a week.

But the drug dealer next door to Honnie and Todd is not rolling over so easily. After the crack house closed down, thereby eradicating a big part of his customer base, he placed speakers in his widows and played Master P's rap song "Snitches" continuously, at ear-bleeding decibels.

Then he set Honnie and Todd's house on fire again. The fire department has taken to sending Honnie the bills for their service, which doesn't help. It also doesn't help that the police, when they came, did not arrest the drug dealer, but Honnie's mother, Bren, instead. The drug dealer had told them that she—Honnie's mother, the lady who makes her own soap—pointed a gun at him and he got one of his crack-addict cronies to corroborate his story, so damn if the police didn't come and arrest that poor lady. She is about as peaceful and sweet as a nun. In fact, she almost is a nun. She's a Baha'i worshiper who would not touch a gun if her life depended on it. *Please*, she brought that asshole drug dealer a basket of homemade soap when they first moved in next door. She and Honnie both offered to assist his girlfriend in enrolling in night cosmetology classes so she wouldn't have to strip anymore; they even offered to babysit their two sad brats if the need ever arose. But then Honnie and her family helped close that crack house down, thereby immensely pissing off the drug dealer next door, and now the police are hauling Honnie's sweet, peace-loving mother off to the hoosegaw based on the say-so of this prick, the guy who *set their house on fucking fire! Twice!*

It's stuff like this that I'd tell newcomers in the neighborhood if they asked me. I'd also tell them about the neighbors who support Honnie and Todd and Bren, too. We all showed up, a crowd of us, at the courthouse when Bren appeared before a judge to answer the charges, and it turned out this same drug dealer had been getting all kinds of people hauled off by the police. He'd just point them out and say he'd been threatened by them, and the police would hone in like hornets to arrest them. A few days prior, the drug dealer had the police arrest the man across the street, a very personable retired electrician for the Ford Motor Company, who supposedly threatened the drug dealer by brandishing a shovel.

The judge dismissed the charges in all cases, but the irony isn't lost on Bren that, while her life is constantly threatened by screaming crack addicts, gunshots, and an arsonist, the police rarely deem it necessary even to write a formal report, yet a known crack dealer can use these same police to cart off unfavored neighbors as though he has all the power of an ill-tempered emperor.

I always drive by Honnie's house on my way home these days because she asked me to. So do a lot of her other friends who live nearby. Other than the drug dealer next door, her street is looking pretty nice now that the crack house is gone. Many houses have been bought up, fixed up, and landscaped. Others show for-sale signs put there by landowners who discovered the neighborhood is starting to pull in prices that make small-time whoring and drug dealing less profitable by comparison. In the middle of it, Honnie's house sits there like a little jewel, with potted flowers on the porch, bullet holes in the window, burned baseboards in the kitchen, and music bellowing from one house over: *"I got a slug for ya'll muthafuckin' snitches. . . ."*

I **PERSONALLY THINK FIFTY IS TOO YOUNG TO DIE,** but Lucky Yates has it all planned out, sort of. He says he wants to be eaten by a snake in the Amazon or something. He wants to go out with a bang, though I don't see how being swallowed whole qualifies. "That's a slow death, not a bang death," I point out, "and being broken down by digestive enzymes has gotta hurt, too."

"Pythons suffocate you before they swallow you," Anna corrects me, but I don't buy that. Who's to say you don't regain consciousness with your body half swallowed? And what if the snake is swallowing you feet first? It's not like you can run away at that point, so you have to just lay there like an idiot with half your body hanging out of a snake's mouth for what could be hours.

"No," I tell Lucky Yates, "please just climb a pyramid in Peru and fall off the top or something." Now that is a good way to go if you ask me. In college I heard about a couple who accidentally did just that, and I remember thinking that had to be the coolest way to kick the bucket this side of being blown apart in the space shuttle. But Lucky Yates is pretty unbendable about the snake.

"I'm not gonna be sitting there in the snake's belly, twiddling my thumbs going 'Hiya,'" he says, smiling with his really white teeth. "I'll be dead, got it?"

That's just it. I don't get it, this whole desire to die young before you become a burden on people. Fifty is downright spry if you ask me. I know plenty of people in their fifties and, goddam, let's just say it would be a real waste to feed them to snakes. That's not saying I myself expect to live much longer than fifty, not that I plan to pitch myself from the top of a pyramid or anything, it's just that people in my family seem to

Out with a Bang

drop like flies after the fifty mark, and I just don't have any experience dealing with relatives who made it into old age.

But I hope I get old. I do. I want to go to the airport every chance I get and be wheeled around like a rickshaw passenger. It might be fun not to feel my feet, too, which I hear is what happens to old people who spent their life not eating right. It might be great to grab onto people as I stumble around. With my job as a flight attendant, I get grabbed a lot by the tottering elderly, and I really don't mind that much. Once it was a ninety-year-old German woman who turned out to be an original Budweiser heiress. I saw her again about two years later, and she remembered me. She had given me her address and wondered why I hadn't written, and I'd have felt bad about causing a rich old lady to await a letter from me that never came, but I was too busy marveling at the sharpness of her brain, and hoping beer played a factor in that.

Then there is Miss Taylor, who lives across the street from me in the crack neighborhood. She is in her eighties and sometimes dances barefoot in the rain, plus she planted sunflowers in her front yard that used to grow so tall they almost touched the rain gutters on her roof. Watching her one morning, I was struck by the difference between Miss Taylor and the memory of my own comparatively young mother, who couldn't even climb out of a car without having to catch her breath. She used to embarrass me, I'm ashamed to admit, especially when she got so ill the only place that would take her was a Tijuana cancer clinic where, for five hundred dollars a day, they specialized in prolonging death once conventional doctors had deemed it inevitable. I used to have to carry her from her bed to the bathroom because she refused to use bedpans. Her habit was to start kicking the second she saw the Haiti-trained doctor coming through the door with a bedpan under his arm. Once she knocked it right out of his hand to the floor, where it clamored loud enough to wake the whole wing.

Now, whenever I wonder if I have the strength to deal with something seemingly insurmountable in my life, I just remember that Tijuana cancer clinic and how I had to cradle my own mother like an infant as her life leaked out of her. Now I know I can face anything, because it's times like these that define you, they serve as a denominator of your character, and I'm grateful my mother bestowed this on me.

But, God, sometimes I'd give it up just to have her back. I wouldn't care if she couldn't dance in the rain, I wouldn't care if there was hardly anything left of her except her colostomy bag connected to her head in a fishbowl, I just really wish she'd made it to old age and was still alive, and whatever burden that might mean to me—or her—I'd gladly bestow it or carry it. I would. But barring that, at least I have the memory of my mother alive and kicking at a Tijuana clinic, knocking bedpans to the floor and going out with a bang.

Bigger Things

THINGS ARE SHRINKING AGAIN, according to Lary. "I'm telling you," he says, measuring random stuff in my house, "things are shrinking." These days he carries a tape measure with him everywhere he goes. He moves to my refrigerator, retractable tape at the ready, and assesses its width, which is the same as it's always been. Everything is the same as it's always been, but that doesn't matter. "Things are still shrinking," Lary says, "including tape measures. Trust me."

Of course I don't trust Lary. This is a guy who, a few years ago, tried to grind black Afghani hash into the pores of my canvas suitcase so I'd be busted by the drug beagle as we came through customs on our way back from Amsterdam. He did not even try to be discreet.

"What the hell are you doing to my suitcase?" I shrieked at him as we sat at the airport waiting to board the plane with the rest of the cattle. But Lary did not even look up. "Your life is lacking drama," he said. I almost missed the flight because I had to hose my bag off at the drinking fountain and then douse it with ten different perfumes from the tester tray at Duty Free. To this day I am still amazed the drug dog didn't sink his teeth into my neck as I came back into the country.

It's funny I should mention baggage, because it's when the airlines got really strict about weighing luggage that Lary became convinced the universe is getting smaller. "Fifty pounds used to be bigger than this," he said, indicating a carry-on bag loaded with his customary airplane supplies, which include Cheetos, white wine, and forged documents declaring him a federally registered child molester. The food and wine are there to keep him from taking hostages in case the plane gets stuck on the tarmac, and the documents are there in case the flight attendant tries to seat him next to an adolescent.

Then he started measuring his cat Mona. But to be honest Mona really was shrinking. Lary actually expects me to feed her while he's away, and he's away a lot lately. One time I opened his door and there was that decayed-flesh smell, and I thought, *Christ, I really killed her this time*, but it wasn't Mona that was dead after all, but a rat she had killed to keep herself alive in between my appearances. After that I was even less attentive, knowing if need be she could subsist on woodland creatures that roam the decrepit mausoleum Lary calls a home.

But Lary has stabilized Mona's shrinking process. It's the rest of the world he's worried about, and he's starting to get me worried, too. Just this morning I was laying there on the bottom part of my daughter's brand new bunk bed, looking at the mattress above me, trying to remember how my sisters and I used to make hammocks when we were kids. First we would take the blanket and tie it to one end of the top bunk and stretch it to the other and secure it somehow. The end effect was a big pocket of sorts, and we would climb inside and hang there like little larvae inside a cotton cocoon. I *loved* doing that. The knots themselves reminded me of a person's head wrapped in a turban, and the hammock their giant tongue.

Anyway, I was looking at Milly's top bunk wondering how the hell we all fit in there, giggling like we did. Surely bunk beds were bigger back then. Everything was bigger back then. The world was just so damn vast and unshoveled, full of mystery and funny turban-wearing people with giant tongues. I remember a big field of mud next to our house, as expansive as the Sahara desert. I used to play in it all day, just mud. Christ, it seems even mud was bigger back then.

That last part is owed to our elderly neighbor named Rocky, who had a Polaroid camera as big as the seat on a bar stool. Once he took our pictures as we played and we got to watch them develop before our very eyes. We were so fascinated Rocky let us keep them. He was always telling us big stories about pirates who used to bury their loot in that very mud field way back when. He'd point to a particular landmark and say things like, "Pirates are notorious for burying their fortunes near crabapple bushes," and we'd rush over there and go digging for it, and damn if we didn't find something every time. I realize now Rocky was burying it there himself. They were pieces of old rhinestone jewelry that probably belonged to his late wife, who I hear had died after cutting her hand on a rusty tin can. Afterward, every week or so, Rocky would scout a new spot and guide us to it, and we'd commence the gleeful process of uncovering new treasure.

Then one day Rocky came by to tell us of a new pirate site, and we simply declined the invite. It's not that we had grown weary of him, it's just that we had grown. When Rocky turned to leave I could see he'd brought his Polaroid camera, and I almost called after him, but I stopped myself. I was on my way to bigger things, I thought, and people on their way to bigger things are too busy to uncover new treasure.

ILL AND MY SISTER CHERYL are down in Nicaragua yelling at each other right now, probably, which is why I'm not looking forward to going there. Cheryl is down there helping him with the small hotel they both now own. Her help and the fact that she offered it so selflessly after Bill's heart attack (if that's what that was) was a gesture for which, over time, I guess Bill didn't show adequate appreciation, because as of now my sister has moved down his street and opened her own business.

"Her crust is getting thicker and I cannot reach her," Bill writes. "Words fall on deaf ears. What fun we're all having, functioning disfunctionally."

"Bill's crazy," my sister had written earlier. "He'll order a hamburger in the restaurant and spit it out on the floor, *in front of the customers*."

Now, I love old Bill, even though he is about as cuddly as a menstruating sea urchin, and I love my sister, even though to this day she will have me in a headlock when the whim hits her (and it hits her about twice daily), but both of them are now imploring me to come to Nicaragua and I'm worried they want me to mediate or validate or something regarding this feud, and, Jesus God . . . I really, *really* don't wanna.

For one, *of course* Bill is crazy. He was living in his car when my mother met him and, showing a judgment of character her daughters would all inherit, became his best friend. He has always smoked like a living chimney, but still his eyes are as big and blue and clear as if they were painted by a preschooler. But there's good crazy and bad crazy, and Bill's crazy borders on good most of the time. He survived being homeless and he survived his supposed heart attack, and he will survive this feud with my sister.

But some survivors are so used to climbing over obstacles that they don't know how to function when their path clears up, so they simply create other obstacles.

Of course my sister's crust is thick. Bill's known her half her life; he helped talk her out of her last bad boyfriend, a bipolar behaving strip-club manager who once embedded all his kitchen knives into the ceiling of her bedroom. Still it took her awhile to give up on that guy, because that girl does not give up on *anything* easily. Even her college education is testimony to that. She didn't get her *degree*, mind you, seeing as how she tests badly, but she's got five years of self-financed, full-time university studies in her brain, which is important.

Anyway, she could have carried Bill out of the jungle on her back if she had to, but Bill didn't need her for that. He needed her to roll up her sleeves and take over, which she did. My sister jumped in with a big belly flop, splashing everyone around, and to her credit some of these people seriously needed some splashing. For example, she saw no use in a kitchen employee who couldn't work a can opener. But like I said, Bill is crazy (although in a mostly good way), and maybe he had a use for that person that isn't evident to your average thick-crusted newcomer. So they yelled about that.

Cheryl also fired the person who functioned as the hotel manager, seeing as how he had a habit of stealing from them and seriously harassing the other employees. But evidently Bill didn't consider these to be bad traits in an employee, so they yelled about that, too.

My only thought is that Cheryl had come there when Bill was sick and infirm with a purpose to clear a path for him as he recovered, and mind you I don't even know if Bill *asked* her to do it, but I suspect a clear path to Bill is like garlic to a vampire; if he can't avoid it he'll destroy it. In this case he did not have to look very hard for obstacles, he simply made one of my sister.

The last time I saw Cheryl it had been a few months since she moved to Nicaragua, and she was visiting the States to attend our little sister's graduation from law school. I think it's always been a touchy subject for Cheryl, her absence of a college degree, and all because she tests badly. After our mother died she moved alone to Las Vegas, and I used to worry about her living there, working an unforgiving job as a cocktail waitress, calling me at 10 A.M. already drunk and bitter, panicking over an army of inner evils, phantom and otherwise.

And Christ, did I worry when she moved to Nicaragua. But when I saw her when she visited last, her arms were toned and her skin was the color of caramel. She complained about Bill, and she smoked like a living chimney but her eyes were big and clear and green. "I've never worked so hard in my life, Holly," she laughed, and I thought about how good it was to see this girl again. I hadn't seen this girl—I mean *this* one, with the easy laugh and the absence of panic—for over a decade. Bill is testing her, yes, but he better watch out. This time she is not testing badly.

HIS IS HOW UNOBSERVANT I AM: I did not even *notice* the lady was naked from the waist down. I mean, Christ, how many half-naked women sitting five feet from your car outside in the cold would *you* fail to spot? Probably not many. But to be fair to myself, it's not like I overlooked her, I saw her right away as I pulled up to park at the church where Milly's preschool is located. The lady was sitting behind a chain-link gate that stood butt flush with the sidewalk, traversing a small concrete easement between two buildings. The lady was right up against the fencing, facing the sidewalk, looking like—and I don't want to be disrespectful—but she looked like a placid creature in a cage. Like I said, I noticed her right away; I noticed her eyes, big and bleak, her hollow cheeks and the concave of her upper lip from the absence of teeth. I noticed how she was shivering, and I noticed her bare, bloody feet, I just didn't notice her poor little bare ass is all.

Besides, church is the last place you'd expect to find a half-naked lady, right? It's also probably the last place you'd expect to find me for that matter. I have gone to church maybe four times on a whim in my entire life, but one thing I noticed while there was that people were pretty well dressed, with hats and everything. My child's preschool, the one that eventually admitted her, thankfully, happens to be attached to a church, but other than that it's a secular establishment. I was a little worried at first about the church thing, but when I set foot in there and didn't burst into flames, I figured it would be fine. Today I have to say I am mighty proud of myself for picking Milly's preschool. She has friends of all religions and races, and at two she could speak Spanish—okay, to be truthful all she can say is *aqui*, but that's pretty damn great if you ask me. When I was her age my biggest trick was fetching beer out of the fridge for my father.

Anyway, this preschool and church are located in the city, and evidently half-naked homeless people are more likely to end up there—trapped behind a locked gate in what amounts to be little more than a concrete crack between two buildings—than they would if these buildings were located in a suburban cul-de-sac. That is just something I knew going in, but still it's surprising when you see it.

"She's cold," Milly said, pointing to the lady behind the gate. I did not need to be told. We tried talking to her, but her response was incoherent. So I told her I'd be right back and took Milly to class. When I returned I saw the church's pastor, Suzannah, unfastening the cumbersome padlock that secured the gate. Until then the half-naked lady had been trapped back there, and we still don't know how she got in there short of climbing the chain link, and she didn't look in any condition to shimmy. I could see my friend Fred walking toward us with a cup of tea he had bought at Kelly's on the corner. Fred's boy, Jake, is one of Milly's best friends. He is a large, handsome child with eyes like liquid Christmas lights, all bright and inviting. Fred handed the tea to the half-naked lady, who promptly spilled it on her feet. Her feet looked just about frozen, so this could have been on purpose.

We discerned that she probably had hypothermia, seeing as she must have spent the night outside in below-freezing weather, so an ambulance was called. In the meantime, another cup of tea was delivered and spilled on her feet, and her pants were found, marking the moment I finally figured out she was naked from the waist down.

I guess until then my brain was just filling in the blank where her pants should have been, offering her a dignity that didn't exist at that particular moment but was hopefully bound to return. And it did. Suzannah helped her into her pants, and then she did something that I personally am ashamed to admit I would not have done. Suzannah put her arms around the lady—her whole arms—and tried to rub some warmth back into this lady's poor hide.

For some reason I was really relieved to see that there are people braver than me, brave enough to be that kind to a crazy, bare-assed homeless person with bloody feet. Fred said so, too. He said that he was worried he'd be admonished for offering her the tea, worried there was a kind of "don't feed the animals" mentality regarding homeless people in this neighborhood, because there is that attitude in other neighborhoods, believe me, mine in particular. I was once subjected to total public humiliation by a coffeehouse employee, who yelled at me from across the courtyard for ten minutes because I gave a buck to a beggar. "They're like puppies, they'll just keep coming back!" she hollered, and I had to slink away, chastised. But now here Suzannah was restoring my faith in humanity by holding this shivering, incoherent, half-naked homeless lady in her arms, holding this person with her whole arms until nobody was half-naked anymore.

I **SWEAR,** Lary's cat cannot die in my own damn house, especially after I made a big show of kidnapping her from him for her own sake. I had to shove her all hissing and wailing into the front seat of my car, because the kidnapping idea came to me spontaneously, after I finally got fed up with forgetting to feed her at his place.

"You hear that?" I yelled at Lary, holding the cell phone up to Mona's howling. "Your cat's coming with me. She's not spending another day all alone in that big damn mausoleum you call a house while you're somewhere else."

At that time Lary was working in New York, probably clinging to a carabiner attached to the top of a stadium that very second, adjusting stuff or whatever it is he does. None of us really know what he does. All I know is that back in the nineties he used to work adjusting stuff locally at rock concerts and we got in free. He'd just walk us in through the back stage, waving at everyone along the way. Once Peter Garrett of Midnight Oil slapped him on the back in passing. "Hey, Otis," he said.

"Who's Otis?" I asked.

"I am," said Lary.

Okay, a lot of people, I suppose, let their brain go to a different place when they're punching the clock, like once I asked my coworker why she was so smiley what with the plane lurching in turbulence like it was being batted around by a big kitten in the sky, and her answer was, "I'm somewhere else. I'm on a sailboat in the Caribbean." So I see how people might mentally transport themselves for a bit when stuff gets a little unbearable, but to create a whole other identity? And Lary's job is not even unbearable. Not to him, anyway. He gets to show up hung over, lug stuff, hang from a harness, and come within a molecule of electrocuting himself. That's what he does at home for fun.

So it's not like he's unhappy, which is the biggest reason I can think of for imagining yourself somewhere else. I remember my family driving across the country in a Ford Fairlane with no air conditioning or seat belts, and the radio didn't hardly work, either, except to bleat out a few notes here and there, making Hank Williams sound like the voice of grownups in the Charlie Brown cartoons. We drove through the desert like that, down Route 66, with both my parents wearing homemade hats fashioned from cut-up Budweiser cans and blue yarn.

At first I wanted to toss myself from the Fairlane's perpetually rolled-down window onto the Santa Fe train tracks that ran alongside the highway, except I was blocked in on either side by my sisters. It was our practice to fight at every rest stop over who'd have to sit on the middle hump in the backseat and it seemed I lost every goddam time, because I recall sitting in that potential shredded-windshield-meat seat for *decades* until I finally figured out how to send my brain somewhere else.

Where I sent it is still a surprise to me, because up until then I'd had only two obsessive thoughts in my head; the first one involved my conviction I was suffering symptoms of every disease I'd been taught about in seventh grade Life Sciences class (including, but not limited to, sclerosis of both the arteries and liver), and the second thought involved Satan and my certainty that he'd possessed my soul.

It did not help that the year before I'd read *The Exorcist*, a book (*with pictures from the film!*) my mother had left lying around like a bottle of prescription drugs for me to fuck with. After that I knew Satan was inside me looking for an orifice to pour out of, and I just tried to make sure there were places I could discreetly duck into once I could feel him about to roil his ugly head. Above anything else, I was more terrified of having to puke and piss in public.

Those were the only two notions I thought crowded my head,

but once we got on the open road my brain didn't take me there, it took me somewhere else entirely. For some reason I constantly found myself on a Ferris wheel pining for an Australian carnival worker who took my tickets at the Myrtle Beach Pavilion. I must have ridden that Ferris wheel fifty times just so I could feel him latch my barrier strap and hear him tell me to have a good ride. He had brown hair to his shoulders, a chipped tooth, and eyes the color of caramel apples. After awhile he just let me stay on board, too, and it wasn't until we heard my father shouting at me from Wump-a-Weasel that he halted the ride to let me off.

So that is where my brain took me on this road trip, thank God, because otherwise I don't think I could have survived the constant worry about barfing up a nest of snakes onto my parents in the front seat. Instead I was somewhere else, I was on a Ferris wheel, falling in love every five minutes. I was hearing my caramel-eyed carnival worker tell me softly, "Have a good ride."

LARY'S CAT WAS TOLERABLE for exactly five weeks, which really faked me into thinking that deep down she was a normal animal and it, of course, was Lary and his influence that caused her to be the demon he'd always claimed she was. Five weeks, I tell you.

"Jesus God!" I shrieked at Lary over the phone. "Your cat all of a sudden, without warning, just turned into a total liquid shit bomb! Not only that, she's stalking my cats! Stalking them like a panther in the wild!"

"I told you," Lary responded smugly. He'd warned me when I'd first kidnapped Mona from his place, after I'd become tired of forgetting to feed her there during his long absences this summer, that Mona embodies a very special kind of evil. "It's been dormant until now. All that shit is to signal you to the presence of Satan."

Most of my house has mangled hardwood floors, so normally this would hardly be a problem, since I could just hose the place off, but Lary's cat had gone out of her way to pick out the sparsely carpeted parts to crap upon, among other places, and we are not talking the kitty Tootsie-Roll turdlettes you would normally expect. No, Lary's cat took the past five weeks to internally brew this special nuclear feline diarrhea with a unique nostril-eating odor, and she took her little cat asshole and splattered my entire place with it like stucco.

On top of that she is tormenting my other cats, Lucy (who is sixteen years old, toothless, infirm, and hardly poses a threat) and Tinkerbell, who is shy and trepidacious, probably because she experiences post trauma from her childhood, when I played a game with her I liked to call "Circus Geek." I'd still be playing this with her today, only she's grown now and her head doesn't fit in my mouth anymore. So Tinkerbell has issues, but at least her behavior is dependable. Lary's cat, now, is a different story. She is entirely capable of passing as a sane animal for large stretches of time, after which she'll erupt without warning into a volcano of crap and madness.

I consider this rare in an animal, whereas with humans this type of personality switch is common. I once met a French guy in Nice named, I swear, Pierre. We were on a train to Paris to watch the Eiffel Tower light up for some celebration, I forget which; all I know is that when we got there Pierre was an angel and I was under his wing and wanted to stay there. When it was time to leave him and return to the States, I cried the big kind of sobs reserved for young military wives at wartime.

"We will see each other again," he whispered to me with the sad accent of a deposed king. The moon was full and my heart was heavy with a longing that, I swear to God, I thought would rip me in half, and he was right. We saw each other again.

Without warning he came to Atlanta soon afterward, and I learned the first of many valuable lessons regarding European visitors, and that is they come to stay not for a few days or even a week, but for as goddam long as they goddam can. After a few months I tried to break it to him gently that maybe he ought to get the hell out of my life for a little bit. We were at a restaurant in Buckhead, as I was hoping the public surroundings would stave any theatrics on his part, but I was wrong.

Without warning he stood, clutched his chest, and began to wail like a sick sea elephant, spouting all kinds of gibberish between sobs. "My father hated me and my mother wanted to abort me!" He howled, clutching at his hair. Luckily, his accent was so thick I don't think anyone really understood what he was saying, but still he was flailing around like an albatross on the end of a harpoon, and all I could think to do was leave.

But Pierre followed me, insisting all the way home that I was honor bound as his hostess to continue our relationship. "I am your *guest*," he kept hollering. "Do you understand? Your *guest*."

But the thicker his histrionics the more steely my resolve. "I want you gone by tonight," I said evenly.

I walked into my home without looking to see if he followed, which he didn't exactly. Instead, he veered into the bushes along the wall of the house, and there he wallowed in the rain and mud, howling and blubbering, tearing at his own clothes. "The more I love you the more you push me away!" he cried.

I ended up calling the police to have him escorted away. I remember handing the officer Pierre's small bag of belongings as Pierre sat in the backseat of the police car, calm now, looking into my eyes, searching for some sign of the woman I was in Paris, the woman who clung to him like stray strips of cellophane. He thought he could find her in there somewhere, behind the hard-eyed statue with arms akimbo that had taken her place. Pierre continued to stare, beseechingly, but that girl was not there. Without warning, she had gone.

SERIOUSLY, I THOUGHT my days of stumbling across bodies on the side of the road were over. Not that my life has changed all that much lately, as if now it's at a point less agreeable for dead strangers to be dumped near me—because my life has *never* been agreeable to that—I just thought I'd seen my share, that's all.

Each time I was in my car, and the dead people were just there, on the side of the road, within cigarette-butt flicking distance. They themselves were not in cars, though I suspect one of them may have been hit by one, hence causing her present state of deadness. But in any case, all of these corpses were just alone in the open air—I mean, aside from one or two well-meaning citizens or MARTA officers waiting for the police to arrive—with no wrecked cars or bicycles nearby to explain their state, lying on narrow, crowded roads in Atlanta neighborhoods.

In the instant I came along, none of the corpses were to be avoided easily, and the first things I noticed were their shoes. I don't know why their shoes always strike me; maybe it's the thought of the dead person having gotten up that morning to put them on like any other morning, not knowing they wouldn't be the ones to remove them that night, not knowing this would be the day they were due to die alone on the side of the road.

I think people who know they're gonna die put their shoes on differently every day. My mother, for example, knew her days were numbered, and she made sure that every morning her feet were covered in the kind of socks she liked, with a short cuff that was tight around the ankle and didn't have to be folded down.

My father, on the other hand, put his shoes on the day

he died just like it was any other day. The shoes were chunky-heeled, cream-colored loafers with buckles across the tops, I kid you not. He put them on and walked out the door to meet the day like he had a million more before him. I don't know why, but for me, the bigger tragedy is caught up in the not knowing.

"Milly, look at me," I say sweetly to her in the backseat as we approach the dead man, his feet splayed at odds to the curb. He's wearing complicated sneakers, the kind with shoelaces *and* Velcro. I adjust the rearview mirror to reflect my face in Milly's direction. "Look at me, honey." I repeat, because I don't want her to be looking at the side of the road. "Look at me and tell me a story."

I love Milly's stories. They have no beginning or end, they're just a farraginous montage of lovely little sentences. Her wishing-well wishes have the same quality. At Fellini's the other day, she'd taken the stack of pennies I gave her and recited one word each as she plunked them into the fountain; "Mommy." *Plunk.* "Mandy." *Plunk.* "Miss Yvette." *Plunk.* "Madelaine." *Plunk.*

"Aren't you gonna to make a wish?" I asked.

"I'm wishing for my friends," she said, and on she went, reciting the names of the people she loves. "Cameron." *Plunk.* "Jacob." *Plunk. . . .*

I don't even know what that *means* and it makes me want to lie down and cry with pride. So imagine her stories. One night, driving along, she excitedly commanded, "Look at the moon!" I couldn't find it at first, but she kept directing me, "Over there! Over there!" Soon there it was, the glorious moon, parting the evening darkness like a tiny slit in a dim blanket pitched over the atmosphere.

"Do you see it? Do you see the moon?" Milly asked, and yes, I saw the moon. What a sight, a lovely crescent-shaped rip that let the light in through the night sky. "Good," Milly finished softly, "because I made it for you."

That, folks, is the day my daughter hung the moon.

"Look at me, honey," I tell Milly as we pass the dead man on the side of the road. "Tell me a story."

"Okay," she says. I can see her face in the rearview mirror, and she's looking at my reflection, thank God. "You feel that?" Milly asks, and yes, I feel something. It's a happy tapping on the back of my seat.

"What is that?" I ask in that hyperexcited way parents talk to their kids when they're trying to distract them from something.

"It's my feet! My feet! My feet!" Milly squeals, laughing. "My feet are *singing!*"

Her feet have been singing ever since we found her a pair of gold plastic slippers at the thrift store months ago. She puts them on in the morning and they don't come off until she's asleep at night, when I creep in and take them off myself.

"My feet are singing!" Milly continues to laugh. "My feet are singing!" Tap, tap, tappity tap tap on the back of my seat. When we're past the dead man on the side of the road, Milly's feet continue to sing, and I have to adjust the rearview mirror again, because now it's my face I don't want my daughter to see.

DANIEL'S AUNT ERMA had an oil well right outside her house. The kind that was always pumping, "so she always had a lot of money." He was telling me about her the other day, his memory having been stirred by the sale on pomegranates at the Buford Highway Farmer's Market.

"Is this the same aunt who had a life-sized replica of Venus de Milo in her living room that lit up?" I asked. I liked that aunt, she always wore wigs, and we are not talking just any wigs, we are talking the kind that look like a yellow cotton farm exploded on your head, with a ribbon in the middle.

No, this was a different aunt all together. In fact, Aunt Erma was not even really an aunt, but his mother's cousin. She was like an aunt, though, a benevolent old aunt who collected husbands like cards in a poker game and kept her diamonds in the freezer and didn't bother to keep it secret, either, pulling them out at every chance and joking about her "ice box." The diamonds might not have been all that valuable, anyway, as one of her husbands had mined most of them himself, right outside the house, and they were big and yellow and mounted garishly.

And Daniel remembers the pomegranates. She had a pomegranate tree in her backyard, and Daniel and his brother Darell would always head straight for the ripened fruit fallen at the trunk, and that is where I like to envision them both; barefoot at the base of a tree, feasting on pomegranates with their Aunt Erma's ugly oil well pumping overhead and unearthed diamonds buried beneath.

It must be memories like this that pull you through. For example, Daniel works teaching art to inmates at a children's mental hospital. He doesn't talk about it much, except to say he is seriously waiting for the day he might find diamonds in his own yard. Or oil. Or something. I don't know. Neither of us do. All I know is that when Daniel sees pomegranates on sale at the Buford Highway Farmer's Market he is saved, for a moment or so, from a rough spot; from the painful longing of something outside his reach right now. He is transported from the faces of the kids he hopes he is helping but can't say for certain he is, to that place under a tree in the Texas sun, laughing and eating pomegranates until the juice ran down his arms in a web of red streaks.

I have a memory like that. It's a glimpse back to my brief period as a pyromaniac when I lived in Melbourne Beach, Florida, while my mother worked at NASA on the last Apollo moon launch. At the time it seemed that every third block or so there'd be acres of untended land that wove through the neighborhoods, rife with pointy plants, sand spurs, and pine trees. My friends and I would burrow ourselves deep within these places, certain we were safe from interference from the outside world, and we were probably right. Not even homeless people wandered into these rough spots, or not for long, anyway.

I was nine and smoking a half a pack a day. Not only that, but I was providing my friends with cigarettes as well, because my parents' habits were so vociferous and they kept such a surplus supply of Marlboros that they never noticed a pack or two missing each morning.

So at first we were foraging ourselves into the rough spots so we could smoke cigarettes undetected every day, but we were nine, so it was just a matter of time before we turned our attention from burning our lungs to burning the wild growth around us. We lit fires like tribal warriors but they never got out of hand, probably because it rains every five minutes in Florida.

The rain, though, now *that* would get out of hand. I remember hanging out in one of these rough spots with my friends when all of a sudden the sky turned gray and began to boil, I tell you, and the wind was so stiff we had to hang onto the trunks of pine trees. High up in the air, above everything else, the tips of the trees were whipping around like kelp at the bottom of an active ocean bed.

I wish I could say it was my idea to climb to those tips, but the truth is I don't know who thought of it. It's possible it could have been a collective stroke of genius, because here we were a bunch of chain-smoking nine-year-olds anyway, so it's obvious life held no value for us, but whatever the case this is what happened. Soon we were each clinging to the tip of our own pine tree and sailing through the air like total trapeze artists, laughing so hard we could barely keep our grip.

Jesus God, looking back I'm surprised I survived. But somehow I was saved, and I'm glad I was, because to this day, when I reach a rough spot in my life, I look back on that moment and I am saved again, by the vision of kids clinging to the tips of trees that had come alive in the wind. Kids laughing in the rain and soaring through the storm.

NEXT WEEK I get to learn how to kill people, and I can't wait. Not that I'm itching to slaughter folks at random, just those who are evil and have it in their head to kill me or others whose welfare I might happen to care about in that instance—the instance of the dangerous uproar. I'm looking forward to acquiring certain techniques that can stop these people, pretty definitely, once it becomes evident that such an instance is at hand. Should it happen, I don't want to be standing there slack-jawed, as useful as a plankton-eating ocean slug. No, I want to be able to kill people in the name of airline security.

I've taken self-defense courses before, but that's just what they were, *courses*. This is not a course, this is *training*. I'll be in training to be a bad-ass, and I'm supposed to expect to be bruised during training, too. I don't care, I grew up being pummeled by every member of my family except my little sister, who was still bigger than me but just didn't have it in her to hurt people. So bruises are no big deal. I got hit by a car in Costa Rica once, which bruised me up really good, but still I didn't plunk down wailing over it. I was embarrassed, is all, to have found myself all of a sudden rolling around on the hood of a stranger's car.

After that I walked back to my *pensione* and promptly got bit in the leg by a black dog, which looked to be part pit bull and part ancient troll roaming the earth under an evil curse. Its teeth were as long and pointy as cayenne peppers, and they left a bloody blossom of gnarled flesh on my upper thigh. That there is testimony to my fortitude, I say, because I continued with my visit even though I was all dog-bit and car-hit, and only missed one day of work after I returned to Atlanta not because of my injuries, but because of the misguided conviction that I'd acquired a tapeworm during my travels.

So I like to think I'm tough as Teflon. For example, when I was eight, my sisters and I were accosted by bullies on our way home from the county fair, where I'd excelled at a carnival game by throwing baseballs at stacks of comical dolls molded from what must have been melted bowling balls, they were so weighted. Still, I knocked enough down to win a stuffed snake, the kind with glued-on eyes and a wire inside so it could bend. The bullies tried to take it from me that day, but instead I thwacked the boss bully upside her head with it and ran away while she gripped her own ears, stunned. Her two minions took off after me, but it was one of the few times in my life when I couldn't be caught. It's a great recollection, but I fear the next time I'm threatened I'll have more at stake than a stuffed snake.

Hence the training. I have it in my head the only element missing to keep me from feeling completely secure is the ability to kill a person with a Q-tip or whatever. If I were brawny I would feel secure all the time, as brawny people all seem to feel, and I wouldn't need to train in order to uncover secrets to survival for the physically meek. I would just rip the assailant's brain right out the back of his skull, or threaten to do so, as I've heard a brawny boyfriend of mine once threaten, and for him the mere threat is always effective enough. I am not him, though.

"You can't kill a person with a Q-tip," I've been informed by various members of certain security forces within the past half year, not even if you swab the Q-tip with rattlesnake venom. But still there must be some other simple-yet-deadly methods of self-defense, some MacGyver moves I can use to murder actively murderous people. When I fly I've taken to wearing my hair in a twist secured by a fancy lacquered chopstick. It's plastic (the chopstick) but it would probably hold up if I had to stab someone in the eye with it.

"Girl, you've got issues," Grant tells me, but he's hardly one to talk. Recently he personally tracked down the thief who took his moped, and wasn't satisfied until the police arrived to slam the guy down and handcuff him right there on the floor of the Ponce de Leon public library. Still Grant thinks I am too enthusiastic about my upcoming training; "Issues," he repeats.

He might be right, because I have not felt secure in a long while. Looking back, I realize even when I clouted that evil cow with my carnival prize it only facilitated an escape for me and not my sisters, who were left behind to be terrorized. I always felt bad about that, and today I figure there's no point in protecting myself unless I can protect others. I can't help it, I want everyone to be safe, and until that happens I guess I will always have issues about security.

True Nature

I **F I HAD A** penis like Matt's I'd probably have it hanging out all the time, too. I'd probably wave it around like a concert conductor every chance I got, which pretty much sums up what Matt does. "Matt had his dick out again last night," Grant says.

"Really?" I say, perking up.

"Yep, he was standing at the end of the bar, I glanced over and there it was."

Grant's seen Matt's dick seven hundred times, starting from way back before Grant began bartending at the Local, whereas I've only seen it less than half that much, so the sight still holds novelty for me.

"How's it lookin'?" I ask Grant.

"Like it's carved out of marble."

I like to think Matt's dick-wag fervor started five years ago when he began hanging out with Grant—who is famous for corrupting people and calling it "the search for truth"—though the truth is Matt may well have been corrupted beforehand. After all, Matt had been robbing banks for a long while before any of us ever even met him.

But Matt likes to point out that he wasn't the guy who actually went *into* the banks with the fake bombs and whatnot. Rather, Matt just provided getaway transportation for the gang, got it? But that still makes him a bank robber according to the FBI, which I'd say is a pretty important distinction. They threw him in jail, but he was out again before I got around to visiting him. I felt bad about that until Grant told me Matt hadn't wanted visitors. Matt has been out for a while now, back to wagging his dick on impulse. "Same ol' Matt," Grant says.

"Let's hope so," I say.

The truth is Matt wasn't the same. For one, he worked out while he was in prison, almost every day from the looks of it, and his body was as buff and smooth as polished pine. He still looks like an angel and probably always will, but now sometimes he also looks like he wishes people wouldn't fall for the act so easily.

Well, it's hard not to. That act is his second nature (as vastly opposed to his true nature). The first time I saw Matt he was holding a puppy. Yes, a puppy. He was sitting on the stoop outside the apartment of my friend, who lived down the hall from me. His hair was long and blond, pulled back in a ponytail, and his eyes were the size of coffee saucers, blue like the Caribbean Sea. When I looked at him it was all I could do to keep from falling over and foaming at the mouth. The puppy really didn't help, either.

"Sarah," I called my friend later, "did you know there's a blond god sitting on your doorstep?"

She did. Later he moved in with her, then after that he moved across the hall from her, and somewhere in between he met Grant and portrayed the crucified Jesus in Grant's art installation at Mary's in East Atlanta in 1998.

Matt had been a bank robber for about two years by then, but even so, out of the gaggle of Grant's friends, he was still probably the best qualified to play Jesus. If not for him, Grant might have had to use Lary, who has long blond hair as well, but Lary is a fermented, misanthropic old lunatic who can't hide his true nature. Matt, on the other hand, was expert at it.

For Grant's opening, Lary had custom built a massive wood cross with a step shelf for Matt's feet and big pegs to which Matt's hands were tied. For five dollars, Grant would provide you with a Polaroid of yourself next to Matt under a sign that read, "Hang with Jesus!" Matt wore pretty much nothing but a big thistle crown and large drops of fake blood. At first there was a whisper of a cloth covering Matt's loins, but I hear that soon fell away and nobody bothered to re-drape it.

That night, a bond formed between Grant and Matt that endures to this day, and sometimes I wonder who is the poorer influence on the other. Before Grant, Matt was pretty good at hiding his true nature, but before Matt, Grant was pretty certain nobody's true nature was worth hiding.

"Do you kiss men?" Grant says Matt drunkenly shouted at him across the bar one night. "Because I can't do that, you know, kiss a man."

Grant and Matt have kissed each other roughly five million times, even more than Matt and I have kissed each other, but this is owing to our days as neighbors, and all that kissing just seemed so innocent. Then I moved away and Matt went to jail and emerged with a harder body, among other things.

"Hang with Jesus," Grant laughs, "because Jesus is *hung.*"

If Grant had a bell at his bar, he'd ring it every time Matt unzips his pants—and the bell would constantly be ringing, and pretty soon patrons would be clutching their bleeding eardrums. So, like everyone, Grant simply allows Matt to drop his act on occasion, because Matt looks too much like an angel for his own good. He can act like one, too, but at least he's not such a shit as to allow people to fall for that act without flashing them a clue, now and again, to his true nature.

NEED PROFESSIONAL HELP. I mean serious help. My
fag friends are of no use to me now, as they're always conveniently invisible when actual elbow
grease is in order. When Grant came by the morning
after Milly's big birthday party, he didn't even bother
knocking. He just peeked in the window and saw the
Chernobyl inside, then scrambled back to his car like a
cowardly crab, the big pussy.

Lary had stopped by Milly's party on his way out of
town again. He handed her a purple stuffed mermaid and
assessed the kiddie-party chaos in progress.
There must have been sixty people
there, and the floor was an absolute
ocean of shredded wrapping tissue
and half-masticated cookies mixed with
fruit punch and Polynesian chicken bits. It didn't help that
I served mai tais, either. Not to the *kids*, of course, but
there was a luau theme, dammit, and I wanted the adults
to have fun, too.

And they did. By the end of the night, the inflatable
palm tree had sprung a leak, the kids were making forts
out of my furniture and some of my so-called adult
friends were in the front yard brandishing my tiki torches
like angry villagers from a Frankenstein movie.

But the worst part was the piñata. A toddler trying to
bust a piñata with a stick is like a fisherman trying to kill a
whale with a fondue fork—I mean, sure, it's *possible*, but
it takes *forever!* So in the end we just put the piñata on
the floor and let the kids tear it apart with their teeth and
hands like little pit bulls pouncing on a pork chop. Disembodied papier-mâché piñata pieces flew willy-nilly, along
with candy and gum and other rainbow-colored crap to
make the paste on my floor complete.

Before leaving, Lary patted my back in an uncharac-

teristic gesture of sympathy. "You don't have to feed my cat tomorrow, if that helps," he said, figuring I'd be too busy wallowing
under all this waste like a bovine trapped in a tar pit.

He was right. It's been five days and I haven't even scraped the
teriyaki sauce off the ceiling yet. I was born without that house-
cleaning chromosome most people take for granted. If it weren't
for my friend Polly the reincarnated putzfrau, who stayed after the
party until midnight washing dishes the old-fashioned way—with
a sponge and water—as opposed to my way, which is one load at a
time in an unreliable ten-year-old automatic from which the
dishes always emerge coated in mystery grit, I would not have one
single piece of tableware left in my entire house, because I seriously would have found it easier to throw all the dirty stuff away
and start over.

This is all pretty pathetic considering I used to actually live
with a maid, which means I wasted a good chance to learn something. I was seventeen and had moved to New Orleans on a whim
and ended up rooming with my hotel's maid when I ran low on
money. Her name was Shirley, and she kept her afro in a scarf during work hours, but at night she shook it loose like a daffodil. She'd
lived in New Orleans for years but had never been to Bourbon
Street, so I took her to Gunga Din's one night, where the motley
female impersonators entertained the audience in their ripped
fishnets and gave detailed descriptions of their upcoming sex-
change operations. We sat in the middle of it all and laughed.

After that Shirley refused to charge me rent, which was a good
thing since I'd just lost my job waiting tables at the Gazebo in the
French Quarter. I don't know what I would have done if not for
Shirley. She was twenty-six and kept her head above water by
cleaning toilets at a low-end hotel, and she wouldn't have taken my
money even if I had it. I was a slob back then, too, and Shirley
would occasionally peek her head in my door, exclaiming, "What a
great mess."

Finally the day came when it was time to leave for home and

finish high school. My mother sent me a ticket, and Shirley dispatched her grudging boyfriend to drive me to the airport in his stolen car with the steering shaft ripped open. Before leaving, I stood with Shirley in front of the house she'd shared with me, hugged her goodbye and told her I'd write. "You ain't gonna write," she laughed, but I insisted I would. She looked at me seriously then, her hair glistening abalone in the sunlight. "You ain't gonna write," she repeated, "but that's okay."

I didn't write. I was seventeen and hadn't yet learned what a waste it is to let good people fall from your life like petals from a fragile rose. I wish I'd written Shirley. I wish I could take her hand right now and lead her into my world, show her the great mess that is my life at the moment, so we could sit in the middle of it all and laugh again.

THANK GOD FOR GAY MEN, otherwise the burden would fall fully on us women to gratify the insatiable male need for sweaty buffalo sex, and I personally don't have the time anymore.

I mean it's not like I'm still in college, which was back before all the really good-looking guys my age figured out they were gay. I was immersed in my pastime of being a blazing four-star slut—or at least I'm pretty sure that's what I was, because it's all a fog and I'm basing this on the rumors I spread about myself. But still, if classmates saw me today they'd be damn disappointed. "What *happened* to you?" they'd ask, and in response I'd have to wave them away from the corner where I'd probably be crouching with dried cake batter in my hair or something. "Go away," I'd groan. "I'm *tired*."

Then they'd go away but their question wouldn't. What *happened* to me? How did my appetites get all turned around? I'd chalk it up to oncoming maturity, but Grant is older than me and his sex life runs at a constant hummingbird pace. I get exhausted just hearing him talk. And Lary, who's older than both of us, has women situated all over the world, the latest being a Bulgarian blackjack dealer he occasionally hooks up with in the Bahamas. Her accent is really heavy, so he doesn't always understand her, but he's almost certain that soon after they met he heard her tell him, "Fuck me until my ears bleed," which did much to endear his feelings for her.

"How romantic," I tell him over the phone. He's in Vail for the holidays, humping who knows what all. "By the way," I add, "your cat is dead."

If I continue at this tempo I figure it's just a matter of time before I turn into one of those drunken old cupcakes who hurl themselves at bartenders while they're working because bartenders are trapped back there like zoo specimens, only worse because they're obligated to talk to you in order to get tips. So I better snap out of this, because my theory is that it all evens out in the end. Like you might think you have no sex drive now, but in fact it's always there, building up day after day, and unless you keep your engine oiled you're gonna end up hit by this big rocket of horniness when you're sixty or something, and then you'll have no choice but to troll your daughter's boyfriends like those lecherous old acid vats you see on daytime talk shows.

I don't want to be like that, a horny old hardened hunk of lard asking neighborhood high school boys to help me with hard-to-reach zippers and such. *Yuk.* But that rocket can't help but accumulate if this keeps up, because it never fails that when my head hits the pillow at night I think to myself, "Damn, I forgot to have acrobatic sex with someone today. Better do it tomorrow." Then tomorrow comes and I waste it feeding my friends' pets while *they're* off having sex somewhere exotic. It's not even like I want to hear about it when they come home all flushed and eager to brag. I just wave them away. "If you need me I'll be in the corner with a bowl of cake batter," I say. Really, what happened to me?

It would be cool if I could talk to my mother about this, because until she died I thought she was the epitome of sexual needlessness. She was a Birkenstock-wearing businesswoman who slept in a separate room from my father for half a decade before divorcing him after twenty-five years of marriage, and she seemed completely happy just to have her life to herself for once; her trailer near the beach in southern California, her kids in college, her occasional Friday excursions to Tijuana with her coworkers. Practically manless, she seemed so content to me. Then years later I was rifling through her effects and found a collection of rough drafts for a personal ad she'd placed in the paper. "Do you like walking barefoot in the grass? Holding hands under a tree?

Watching the sunset from a hillside?" they read. The appeals were so achingly sweet, and dripping with romance and longing I'd never known her to feel.

So I guess she got hit by a different kind of rocket, and here I'd never even seen her go on a date, which makes me worry that no one responded to her ad. But I can't bear to leave it at that. I have to hope that maybe someone did respond, and she kept it secret from us, and she got to wiggle her toes in a meadow while holding his hand after all. I have to hope that she found what she was looking for, even fleetingly, and that she didn't spend a single second sitting around alone, clutching an unanswered personal ad, asking herself, "What *happened* to me?"

IF YOU WERE A CONVICTED child-molesting masturbator, I suppose you would need to live somewhere,
I was just hoping it wouldn't be on my actual damn
street. I was hoping, in my small world, all convicted
child molesters could live in prison, maybe, perhaps
bricked up inside a jailhouse toilet or something, not *four
blocks away* from my front door. That's practically ejacu-
lation distance, according to Grant. Lary says I should
shoot the pervert in the head and drag his body onto my
property to feign an intrusion, but that's Lary's answer to
everything. He is always wanting to shoot people and drag
their bodies onto his property.

"Wouldn't it be easier to just lure them inside, then
shoot them?" I ask.

"I'm not alluring," he answers.

Besides, Lary wants to leave a big blood trail for the
police to ignore. Ever since Lary shot at that burglar es-
caping down the street years ago, and the police told him
not to miss next time, he has been itching to test the
boundaries of their complacence. In fact, he's been looking into the Georgia Bureau of Investigation sex-offender
web page himself lately to see if any perverts are living on
his own street within comfortable dragging distance, and
I'm sure there are. But this is all sport to Lary, as he
doesn't have a kid.

I, on the other hand (and fantastically enough), do. I
thought the severed human head in a plastic sack the
police found on my street was bad enough. But no,
there are also the arsonist drug dealers, the
whores (alive and dead), the flying bullets, and
now this child molester. These facts aren't *related* to each
other in any way; I just wanted to illustrate that it's hard
to shake the portensions you feel when you become a

parent while living in a neighborhood littered with body parts *and* perverts.

Surprisingly, though, I've weathered it all, plus the occasional homeless crack addict knocking on my door for a handout, but still I worried almost every day that a good rain would uncover the rest of the severed head's body parts somewhere within crawling distance of my kid, and I discovered that my bedroom had a boarded up fireplace within the wall, as well, which is a good place to conceal a corpse if you ask me, so I kept imagining I saw seepage through the plaster.

Today there are still plenty of homeless people around, but at least the crack factor has been dissipated a little, though 4 A.M. is still crack-whore happy hour here. I know this because once I drove Milly to Children's Hospital in the middle of the night due to a fever I thought was hot as lava, and our neighborhood was boiling with whores at this time, along with addicts and dealers and other dregs of the trade. And then there is that child molester.

Lary has driven by his house a few times. So have Grant and Daniel, if for no other reason than it's hard not to when you're coming to visit me. They're ready to pounce, they say, in case they catch the guy masturbating on a school bus or whatever. At this point, though, all they can do is watch, but at least watching is something.

In the meantime I'm so overcome with a general fear that I can do nothing but simply lie beside my sleeping girl and beg for forgiveness, because often I anguish over the groundless notion that there's some kind of karmic roll-over policy, and that Milly will be made to suffer for my past apathies. And God knows I should have been a better person. I should have been a better daughter, sister, friend, whatever. I should have not stolen milk money from my first-grade classmates, I should have not taunted the neighborhood senile lady when I was ten, I should have—oh, God—I should have not deserted my father the night he died. If I had only done or not done these things, maybe we wouldn't be living down the street from a convicted child-molesting masturbator right now, I would not be worrying about my little toddly woddly girl and how to keep her from the frosty, random fingers of evil that wrest up from the earth and lurk there, ready to rip your heart out from your ribs when, hey, they don't have to go to the trouble after all. Because there your heart is, all bundled up and teetering around *outside* of you, all big-eyed and vanilla-smelling and dough-bellied, with tiny ears like intricate seashells you could stare at all day. There your heart is, smiling and laughing and waving at you from a distance, ready to be plucked like a little button mushroom. All you can do is watch, but at least watching is something.

GIANT MICHAEL IS IMPLEMENTING a no-idiot policy at the Vortex and I seriously don't know how he gets away with it. For one, the Vortex is a goddam bar. I myself have been an idiot in there many a time, the most recent being that time when he first introduced me to the perfect mojito, and then later Red Bull and vodka, which is like liquid crack if you ask me. Why would a friend do that to you? I actually ended up at a fetish nightclub, the Chamber, that night. Here I'd been living in Atlanta for almost the entire life of an Olsen twin, and I had managed to avoid the Chamber all that time. Then that night after being an idiot at the Vortex, I end up at the Chamber in my white work blouse watching burlesque and so wired on Red Bull I could probably set off car alarms across the street if I was concentrating (which I wasn't). "If you discriminated against idiots," I tell Giant Michael, "you'd hardly have any business."

"On behalf of my customers, I'm offended by that," he says, which makes me laugh, because Giant Michael isn't offended by anything. Believe me, I've tried.

Lary and I used to hang out at the original Vortex on West Peachtree a hundred years ago, and we would make it our mission to offend everyone around us, and since the place was so small and Michael is so giant, he was always around us. "Juice me up, booze jockey," I'd demand, thrusting my empty glass at him. He's totally like emotional marble. He's one of my oldest friends and the closest I've ever seen him get to actual angry was today with this whole anti-idiot campaign. He was damn near riled up, blaming everything on the yuppie onslaught of Midtown due to the recent outbreak of condo complexes all around. To Michael's credit, Midtown really does look like a beehive lately, but that's something any normal restaurant owner would be ecstatic about. Not Giant Michael. When I walked in, he was perusing a list of new T-shirt slogans he recently approved for his waitstaff. Among them are: "Your Village Called. Their Idiot Is Missing" and "Don't Make Me Throw You Outta Here."

"We just got a letter from a guy who brought his kids in here and told us he was outraged by the porn we have pinned to the walls," he exclaims with a sweep of his arm. "Porn? Do you see any porn in here?"

Well, I personally wouldn't classify it as porn, but among the immense clutter of vintage signage, toys, motorcycle parts, skeletons, and other oddities attached to the ceiling and walls, there is an autographed picture or two of strippers with pasties on their tits. "That's not porn," he insists, almost riling up again. In the foyer he has just, that day, mounted a collection of framed commandments for customers to follow, basically banning "tight asses, moochers, whiners, oblivious parents, idiots, and drunken idiots" from the premises.

"Aren't you afraid of pissing people off?" I ask.

"What are they gonna do? Come up to me and tell me they're an idiot and they resent the discrimination?" he says, and I have to think about that, because, though I wouldn't want to represent all of idiotkind, I am nonetheless sensitive to my idiot side. I must like to take it out for walks occasionally, because I have done some pretty stupid things, believe me, many of them in bars. I tell them all to Michael, like how, in college during my fake I.D. stage, I was kinda famous for getting drunk and passing out in restaurant bathroom stalls.

"That's nothing," Giant Michael assures me. Then I tell him about the time years ago when I flashed my boobs at a bar in Key West, and he rolls his eyes like I could not possibly be more boring. He approves another T-shirt slogan. This one reads, "I'll Hurt You if I Have To."

Then I tell him about the time, back in my longhaired, silver-ring-on-every-finger stage when I, just for the fun of it, stole my friend's boyfriend just as easily as plucking a feather from the air. All it took was two cocktails and about ten seconds of eye contact and I had him in my hand like lotion. My friend's name was Mary, and I remember she had brown Dorothy Hamill hair and liked to wear boyish shirts with turned-up Oxford collars.

They were new in their relationship, and in the weeks since they'd met, Mary had been incandescent with a glee that I guess I couldn't bear. She had come into the bar clinging to him like sea kelp, all aglow and proud with moon-shaped eyes looking up at him like he was a wonder to behold. I just remember her face that night, her smiling face, and how it fell like a Malibu mudslide when she realized what was happening.

I confess all this to Michael, and I look up at him like he should throw me out right then, because here I am a self-confessed idiot in his bar, but instead he puts his arm around me. "You're not an idiot," he comforts me, "you're a goddam fool," and kisses the top of my head.

FOR YEARS I'D HEARD that the entertainment at the Chamber could be kinky, consisting of public genital piercings performed to a techno beat and such. I mean, it's a *fetish* club, for chrissakes, and until last Friday the closest thing to a fetish club I'd encountered was a fag bar in Prague complete with stalls with holes in the walls that guys could back their asses against in order to have anonymous sex with someone in the next room.

I was with Lary that time, too, as well as Daniel and Grant. It was early in the evening, the stalls were unoccupied, and since Grant was not gay yet it fell to Daniel to explain to us what the holes were for—that and why there were toilet-paper dispensers attached to the bar. Then the bartender kicked us out on account of my being female, and my friends also for having been tainted by such close proximity to my ovaries and all. Lary tried to convince him I was a pre-op transsexual, but the bartender wasn't buying it and ushered us out before I could kill the vibe by waving Kotex around or something.

Anyway, I'd never been to the Chamber before, not even when I was young, so I figured I had no business going there now, all old like I'd been feeling lately. Michael had bought me lunch that day while Milly was safely tucked away with relatives, and since he owns the Vortex bars, to him lunch starts at 5:30 P.M. and consists solely of mojitos and tortilla chips. Mojitos are those Cuban cocktails made with mint, sugar, lime, and rum. I'd fallen in love with them while attending a wedding in Miami last year. But there are bad bartenders down there just like anywhere, and sometimes I'd be handed some vile thing that tasted like a cup of fresh bile mixed with battery acid.

I drank them anyway, and at one point I wandered into a gift store and came across a large book of photos, the sole subject of which was mummies.

All the mummies came from the same crypt in Italy, and it was impossible to pull my eyes away, even when I turned to the page of *child* mummies. They hung like dolls on a wall, all dressed in the Renaissance equivalent of their Sunday best, with ruffled collars and intricately croqueted jackets. It was heartbreaking, to think that so many mothers had to dress her dead children in these treasured vestments so their bodies could be hung for hundreds of years in a cold labyrinth.

My friends had to pull me away, and I finally found the perfect mojito when this little old Cuban lady bartender actually pulled out a *mortar and pestle* when I ordered. You know it's gonna be a good mojito when the bartender uses tools favored by pharmacists and ancient apothecaries. So when Michael told me his bartender, Carla, makes a perfect mojito, I had to scoff, because I'd been graced by the little old Cuban lady. "Does Carla have a mortar and pestle?" I smirked.

"Of course," Michael said.

Four mojitos later I was at the Chamber with Lary and Michael and their two hot girlfriends, waiting to catch burlesque performances. My friend Andy was there with his camera at the ready in case I started waving Kotex around so he could take a picture. He had been cracking me up all week with e-mails about the rat in his house. He'd never actually seen this rat, just the damage it wreaks, so he nicknamed the rat "Chupacabra," after the mythical Mexican beast that mutilates livestock.

The rat made me think of the book of mummies again, because in it there was a picture of a mummified woman who must have died crouching in a corner, clutching her child. Also in her arms was the shriveled carcass of what looked like a rat, but turned out to be a small dog that just looked like a rat in its macerated condition. The mother-and-child mummy cluster sparked an ocean of questions inside me. How did they die? Were they poisoned? Were they killed quickly? Did they languish? Whatever the case, they must have crouched there—this woman and her child and her pet rat dog—crouched there for decades right where they died before being discovered. I keep seeing that picture in my mind, and the baby's fists are balled up under its chin, reminding me of miniature rosebuds in a wedding bouquet.

So there I was at the Chamber, talking to Andy about his rat, surrounded by Lary and Michael and their two hot girlfriends Tatiana and Kristen, watching burlesque and wondering what had happened to the beings that made up the mummy cluster, what could have killed them so quickly or trapped them so unforgivably that the woman had nothing to do but clutch these treasured things and simply expire that way, crouching in a corner. There I was, flanked by my friends, and by the time we left I wasn't feeling so old anymore.

N THE END, Lary did not die. Thank God. I do not need that guilt on my head, though his being dead would not have been my fault entirely. His being dead would have been *his* fault entirely, but I still would have felt fairly bad about it.

"What happened last night?" He asked me the next morning. "Why does the side of my head hurt?"

"You must have hit it when those three guys pulled you out of your car," I suggested. "Or maybe it was when you fell under the sink."

The falling was certainly a possibility, since he was already wobbling by the time he got to the Local, where we all were supposed to be guest bartenders that night to celebrate Grant's last night working there.

I showed up only a little late, because to me, even though I was a "guest," the evening had the ring of work about it, so I took my time getting there. Daniel, of course, was already elbow deep in dishwater by the time I walked through the door. He's a great guest worker. I think I'll tell him I'm having a "guest scullery maid" night at my house, featuring him. He'll show up with his own mop and bucket, I'm telling you.

The occasion regaled Grant, the real bartender, who was working his last night at the Local before embarking on the full-time pursuit of his Sister Louisa vision, and he had the three of us show up to form a kind of celebratory farewell foursome. A treat to his regulars, he said, though in the end I believe I am the one who was treated. They all tipped the shit out of me.

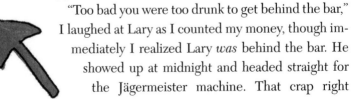

"Too bad you were too drunk to get behind the bar," I laughed at Lary as I counted my money, though immediately I realized Lary *was* behind the bar. He showed up at midnight and headed straight for the Jägermeister machine. That crap right there is enough to kill you if you ask me. It seriously looks like some poison I got into under our bathroom sink once when I was five. Brown sludge with stems and grit in it probably. Why it needs its own dispensing machine is a mystery to me; maybe it's to better protect the person serving it. Lary had handed out a half dozen free shots of the stuff before Keiger, the one who owns the bar, stopped him and declared the Jägermeister machine officially broken, and Lary officially banned from behind the bar.

Ha! Don't ever tell Lary to stay away from a broken thing. It's like telling a kitten to stay away from an open can of tuna. Even drunk, Lary can fix anything—or build anything, for that matter, which might explain the scaffolding that mysteriously appeared in his kitchen last week. Lary claims he doesn't even know how it got there, but I do. I bet there was something broken up there, and Lary was trying to reach it. He'll probably invent time travel one day, because there are broken things all over history, and sooner or later Lary will figure out how to reach them. For example, if he was on the *Titanic*, he could have patched that hole with some indelible paste he made from nail polish and pancake batter or something, and he could have done it shit-ass drunk, too.

So I kind of felt bad for Keiger, because he obviously did not know this about Lary, and it took all of an eye blink before Lary was back on that machine churning out megashots of the stuff until finally he was, literally, under the sink.

"Make sure he does not drive himself home," Keiger told me once Lary found his way back to a bar stool, but by that time I was nearly fogged myself with that night's made-up drink special. It was called the Honky Bitch, and it contained every sugary liqueur to be found behind the counter, with heavy emphasis on Bailey's, and maybe a shot of soda or something. By the end of the night, Keiger looked like somebody shot in the gut, reconciled to the fact that no matter how hard he clutched his wound it wasn't about to stop the bleeding.

Still he tried to keep an eye on Lary, but Keiger only has so many eyes, and Lary is quick, even shit-ass drunk. I remember I was on the phone calling Tatiana, Lary's friend who lives nearby, to come and pick him up when suddenly I heard Keiger holler, "Where the hell's Lary?" We all looked around, even under the sink, but Lary was not there, he was *in his truck*, backing out of the goddam parking lot. "Pull his ass out of that truck," Keiger directed, and three guys ran out and literally did just that. They left his truck right there, too, halfway backed out, and then they stuffed Lary's freckled, Jäger-soaked hide into a taxi.

For that reason Lary is alive today, probably. So in a way I guess Keiger did stop the bleeding that night, even if it was just Lary's useless, crusty reptilian blood. I have to commend Keiger for that, too, because if it were me, and if that were my bar, and Lary hijacked the Jäger machine like he did, I would have left Lary right there where he fell the first time—under the sink.

IF YOU'RE GONNA GET ROBBED, it might as well be by the best, and you'd have to be the best to rob my sister Cheryl. The last time somebody tried to take her purse, for example, not only did the robber not get away with it, my sister chased him down and gave him a concussion just for trying.

But this new thief, he did not take her purse, he took her money belt out from under her clothes, which, believe me, she did not take off, not on a bus in front of a stranger, anyway, and especially not since she moved to Nicaragua and became completely schooled in self-protective travel.

"Oh, he was good. I mean, he was *the best in the world*," Cheryl laughs.

She is always laughing, but even so, her spirits are remarkably high for someone who just lost all the money it took her seven months to save, plus credit cards. She's visiting again from Nicaragua, and she spent her first two days here on the phone canceling everything and retelling the story to the credit-card operators ("This pickpocket was like a *laser surgeon*, I swear!"), and they listened.

It's hard not to listen to Cheryl. She talks at a decibel reserved for fire alarms, and always with the excitement of someone who just won a Winnebago on *The Price Is Right*. At first I worry people will begin to back away like you might do when you realize someone's got a cog missing in their mental mechanism or whatever, and for the first few days of her visits I'm always ready to be her handler or something, to interject with a pert "She's just so happy because she's spent a long time deprived in Nicaragua."

But Cheryl does not need a handler. People love her. We can't even go to the grocery store without Cheryl inviting the cashier to come visit Granada to drink at the bar she owns there, or stay at the special *pensione* down the street from the bar, which she also owns with Bill. Bill is feuding with her hatefully now, but nonetheless he had given her most of the money the thief ended up taking. It was a spontaneous repayment for a long-since abandoned loan.

"Bill's gambling again," Cher sighs, and I nod but I don't know how to take the news, because Bill is a really good gambler. It's one of the things my mother and he had in common. After she died I found a homemade card-counting computer in her effects, one that fit into her shoe that she could work with her toes to produce a readout on a fake watch she wore around her wrist.

When I found that I immediately thought that my mother, who'd spent her adult life designing missiles for the government, had finally found something to do she didn't hate, and I knew Bill had helped her get there somehow. If my mother had been alive when Bill moved to Central America, she probably would have followed him there, so Cheryl went instead.

I haven't been to Nicaragua myself, but judging by Cheryl's elation when she comes back, there is evidently very little there in terms of modern comfort. When Cheryl comes to Atlanta, she is always foaming at the mouth, practically, over things like warm water, for instance, or bread.

"Bread! Bring bread! They don't have bread in Nicaragua!" she shouted gleefully at the waitress at Carroll Street Café her first night back. My sister's eyes are freakishly green. They glow like two tiny nuclear reactions right there on her face. The waitress was really quick with the bread, and my sister tore into it like a wolf on an injured woodland creature.

"They don't have *bread* in Nicaragua?" I asked.

"Not good bread," Cheryl said, her mouth full of bread. "This is the best in the world," she groaned.

It's difficult not to be taken with someone who possesses such an unadulterated lust for everything. A trip to the drugstore, for example, turns Cheryl into such a quaking volcano of joy you just gotta lay down, you're laughing so hard. She flits from display to display, squealing stuff like, "Oh, look! Peanut clusters! They don't have these in Nicaragua! I've been *dying* for some of these!"

I used to think she was crazy, and tried to get Daniel, Grant, and Lary to agree with me, but they are crazy *about* her. Especially Daniel, who's been devoted to her ever since that morning years ago when she made him her special breakfast smoothie, which contained two treeloads of fresh fruit "and my secret ingredient," Cheryl said, emptying half a pint of Bacardi into the blender.

"That's not *breakfast*, that's a goddam *daiquiri*," I pointed out, but Daniel and Cheryl were already on their second helping and I was feeling a bit peckish myself, so I poured myself one. We ended up at the Clermont Lounge that afternoon, with Cheryl becoming best friends with the strippers after gathering their advice on professional beaver-shaving techniques.

Now she's back, her appetites so simple and yet so vociferous—the best kind to have, I guess. "Oh, my *God*," she groans, sniffing something in her hand like it was the last pocket of oxygen on an airless planet. It's a cup of cappuccino. "Oh my *God*," she repeats, and I think I see actual tears of joy in her nuclear green eyes, "this is the best in the world."

Lucy

GODDAM THAT STUPID, lousy cat Lucy. It's not as if she was the nicest cat around, or even the prettiest, what with her upper teeth all gone due to that tumor that took over her face like magma, but she was reliable, at least.

And *moody*. Christ, that cat could psyche in a second. Don't fall for all that purring. She could purr as loud as a lawnmower, but it was just a decoy to get you to reach out to her. Then the next thing you know that cat is wrapped around your hand like an evil oven mitt, all fangs and claws and wild green eyes imbedded in your arm up to your elbow. I hate to think of the damage she could have done if she had all her teeth.

Even so, I became accustomed to that craggy cloud of black-and-white fur looming through all the homes I've had in the fourteen years since I got her. I used to count how many addresses that was, but I can't do that right now. There were just so goddam many, and thinking about them makes me realize how little I've had to rely on regarding continuity in my life. Lucy was not much, but I relied on her in that regard. She was with me almost as long as my own father, but she had the decency to die old for a cat, whereas my father died young for a man.

Recently I flew to San Diego, where I drove to a half dozen other old addresses just to see if they were still there. I don't know why I do that. They are always still there, but whatever elements in them I'd treasured in my memory had vacated, thereby making them barely recognizable. It's no minor heartbreak to barely recognize a piece of yourself, but I kept going from address to address anyway, hoping to find a spark of familiarity. There was none. So I came back to Atlanta, where there was.

Lucy started losing her teeth when she was just a year old, when that bump first appeared on her upper mandible. The vet gave her six months to live, so I took her home thinking I could make the craggy thing comfortable until it was time. Six months plus thirteen and a half years later it was time, but I didn't think so. I kept hoping, you know, maybe she'd rally like she always had. I kept asking people, "How do you know it's time?"

Everyone always said I would just know. I kept waiting to know, but the knowledge didn't come even when she hid in my hamper for three days. That tumor kept getting bigger and bigger, too. She looked like a feline Elephant Man, but so? She'd always been ugly, now she was just uglier. Ugly is no reason to put a good cat down, is it? Then I took her out of the hamper and placed her in front of a bowl of canned peas.

Before I go on I have to say that by the time I'd first laid eyes on Lucy at the Humane Society, she had lived a hard six months of alley life during which I guess food was an uncertainty at best. That uncertainty must have stayed embedded in her feline brain the rest of her life, because she never passed up anything edible that I know of. She could even keep my full-grown pit bull Cookie at bay while she perused the dog food bowl for herself, and don't even try to eat canned peas around her, because she will bat them right off your fork and into her own mouth. There were two occasions long ago when she mysteriously lost weight and withered down to a sack of twigs, but she quickly puffed up again and never lost that craggy sparkle that caused Daniel to conclude Lucy was a reincarnated truck-stop waitress.

But this time, when I put her in front of the peas, it's not so much that she wouldn't eat them, it's that she tried to so unsuccessfully. Watching her lower her weary, deformed face into the bowl, her hide hanging off her bones like laundry, I just knew.

Lucy was ugly and often mean, true, but she still let me hold her close in the night like the pink stuffed poodle I cherished as a child. I don't know if Lucy enjoyed that or tolerated it for my sake, but in either act there is love, and you'd be hard pressed to let it go if you had it.

I made the appointment the next day. Daniel came with me, even though the only pet I've known him to have was a goldfish he "accidentally" ground up in the garbage disposal. He was still the right person to ask, though, because he understands attachment. He just wasn't attached to that goldfish is all.

Lucy handled it perfectly. She lay peacefully on the table, exhausted and purring, and I looked into her wild green eyes for a long while. Then the Lucy-ness simply left her. Whatever elements in her I'd treasured—that spark of familiarity—had vacated. With that gone, she was barely recognizable, and it's no minor heartbreak to barely recognize a piece of yourself.

GRANT, THAT BITCH, has stolen my sister. Or my sister, that bitch, has stolen Grant. Or, goddamit, both those bitches have stolen my life!

They are, at this moment, traveling to New York in Grant's blasphemous Rolling God Box—a retrofitted florist's van covered with typically inspired Sister Louisa sayings like "Jesus Curls His Hair with Holy Rollers," and "Man Made God in His Image,"—and stopping every thirty-three miles to nail signs ("With Jesus nails, of course," Grant insists) along the highway.

Or at least that was the plan, anyway, until they began getting surveilled by police helicopters somewhere around Maryland. But they were able to pick up the sign-nailing pace again once they crossed the Virginia state border, or whatever state border borders the state of Maryland. Along the way they spend their evenings in bowling-alley bars ordering exotic shots and hijacking the karaoke machine, or at least that's what I'd do if it were my life being lived by me instead of being stolen by my sister and my best friend.

Grant will even admit he's never been on a road trip this long, whereas for me the drive from Atlanta to New York would have been a complete cake walk, me being the daughter of a traveling trailer salesman. Of course my sister Cheryl is also the daughter of a traveling trailer salesman, which doesn't help. As the victim of a stolen life, I must say it's no comfort that the theft was able to occur so seamlessly. My father used to drive with both our unbuckled asses in the front seat as we charted the course for him, badly. Peering at the map, we'd advise, "Turn right at the red dot."

Now Cheryl is advising that to Grant, and so far the

trip has been milder than anticipated, even though they made sure to spend as much time as possible traveling through South Carolina. They have not even gotten beaten by police or sodomized by mullet-headed rednecks, as Grant was kind of hoping. What they are getting is flipped off.

"I can't believe that twelve-year-old black girl just flipped us off," my sister bellowed incredulously to me through Grant's cell phone. "What girl? Where?" I ask frantically. Jesus, doesn't she understand I need details if I'm going to live my own life through her?

Because right now I am living someone else's, and I wish the person it belongs to would come back and reclaim it, because this person's life *sucks*. Right now it's steeped in cutoff dates, mean people, greedy pricks, and fear as I try to qualify for a home loan based on my meager income in an effort to move out of this neighborhood. I am so mired in credit checks and other bureaucratic quicksand that evidently my own sister had to come from Nicaragua and impersonate my old self so my best friends could be bookmarked to enjoy at a later date, and for that I guess I should be grateful, but as I said I am not myself. Instead I just look at Cheryl longingly from the life I'm in right now, wondering when I'll get mine back.

"What's wrong with you?" Cheryl kept asking before she left with Grant. She kept trying to sneak alcohol into me, too, hiding it in my orange juice and whatnot, but it's been so long since I tasted booze that my senses are now hyperalert to its presence. I think Lary put her up to it. He is downright pissed at me for not drinking anymore. "Hollis," he said seriously, "if you don't drink, people are gonna think you're an alcoholic."

This is *Lary* here, the guy who is turning his warehouse into a haunted church this Halloween, with bloody flagellated Jesuses pawing at people like plague victims and everything. Since when does Lary care what people *think*?

"Leave me alone, you worthless stain on the butt end of the

earth," I growled at him, which encouraged him a little, like maybe I was starting to come back, but then I fucked that up by bursting into tears.

It's my sister, I tell you. My sister is exhausting me. It's not just because she takes stuff from me, like my life and other things she thinks I won't miss, or because she rearranges all my furniture, or because she filled my cupboards and refrigerator with irresistible food for me that I don't want in my house, like cheddar cheese and potato chips and deep-fried chocolate-covered butter sticks. No, it's because she makes me dinner and tries to be helpful and always wants me to tell her what's wrong with me precisely at the moment I need to pour all my energy into pretending everything's fine.

She just always shows up when there are truths to be buried, and the truth is I am not fine. I am fearful and hesitant lately, and I am buried beneath things I think should be and pinnacles I think I should have reached by now. Like I should not be living across the street from a drug dealer, or down the street from Crack Corner, or in a house with a lawn where whores toss their soiled condoms. My sister has this awful ability to extract these buried truths; they emerge as if pulled by a powerful magnet, pulled out by the roots.

"It's like heart surgery," I tell Grant over the phone, our main mode of conversing lately. "I know I'll be better because of it, but it's fucking painful while it's happening." "THE TRUTH," Grant hollers joyously from behind the wheel of his Rolling God Box. "THE TRUTH SHALL SET YOU FREE." Then I can hear them both laughing as they ride along in my missing life, stopping every thirty-three miles to nail up signs.

I SWEAR, GRANT'S ROLLING GOD BOX has been hardly vandalized at all, but to hear him tell it, you'd think thugs marauded over in droves, with torches and everything, to tear that van apart.

"I am sad to report that the Sister Louisa's Rolling God Box was vandalized across the street from the St. James Baptist Church in Brooklyn where I parked it Saturday night as a Sunday-school lesson for the next morning," he mourned in a mass e-mail last week.

"Someone took spray paint and blacked out the words 'Jesus' and 'God,'" he continued. "I think it was a lesbian crack whore who likes preacher dick, because all *those* words were left alone."

So here I'm envisioning a blackened relic that was once a white van covered in big-lettered Sister Louisaisms—such as "Jesus Loves a Crack Whore," and "God Is Pissed"—limping back to Atlanta with pistons missing and maybe some heavy smoke belching out the ass end, too. But seriously, there are just a few black smudges, and on only one side. Yes, the "Gods" and "Jesuses" were blacked out on that side, but he can put them back easily enough, just paint them right back on top of the blacked-out parts.

"You pussy," I tell him. "A couple of smudges. Big deal."

"But those were perfectly good words," Grant gasps. "Now they're *censored*."

Ha! Like he has never been censored before. I estimate he spent a good 75 percent of his life censored, and I'm being generous. By my estimate, Grant was free a few years prior to his having busted out of the closet at the age of forty-two. I'm figuring he really wasn't all that censored during that time, just undecided about what he wanted to say. When he made up his mind, though, you couldn't shut him up.

"Nothin' Harder than a Preacher's Dick!" the God Box blares in colored lettering along its uncensored side. Grant had driven that thing up to New York "goddam titty-ass" City and back, having spent a month in between trying hard to piss people off everywhere he went. In short, he was new in town and needed attention.

I guess he got it. I personally prefer other means of garnering attention when new in town. In fact, before I came to Atlanta, being new in town was nothing new to me. I'd moved every year of my life, and my method of coping was to blend, literally, into my surroundings. In my second school during my eighth-grade year, for example, I spent every recess hiding in the handicapped stall in the girl's bathroom. This had become my habit ever since the fourth grade, when my father advised me that a good way to break the ice at a new school would be to march right up to the biggest person on the playground and demand, "Who's the head nigger in charge?"

I wouldn't say it was the worst advice, because it got me a lot of attention, just not the kind I wanted. By eighth grade I'd stopped listening to my father, in almost every sense. His way of blending into a new town was to find a particular kind of bar and go there every day. It was the kind of bar that opened at 6 A.M. and was completely devoid of natural light unless someone opened the door to enter, which wasn't that often during my father's favorite hours. The barstools were upholstered in red naugahyde and so was the cushioned bumper around the edge of the counter, where people propped their elbows for their first ten beers, their armpits for the next ten, and then their faces, probably, for any after that. There would be a jukebox, of course, with a smattering of songs by Blood, Sweat, and Tears being its most current offering.

Wherever we moved, my father found a bar exactly like this one. In Costa Mesa it was the Tin Lizzy; in Melbourne Beach, the

Casino; in Nashua, Gino's; in Torrance, the Albatross. In every instance he walked right in, broke the ice, picked a stool, and hardly left until it was time to start packing for a new city again. At every bar the bathrooms were an odyssey of graffiti slogans, and I could sit in them for hours reading the walls.

That is except for the Tin Lizzy, where Kitty, the beehived bartender, had regularly policed the ladies room for graffiti to block out any profanities with a black Sharpie marker. My father liked Kitty fine, even though her nickname for him was "useless sack of crap." I liked her fine, too, because she used to let me take the marker in the bathroom when she was too busy to censor the writings in there herself. I didn't know good words from bad, so I'd emerge from the toilet occasionally to inquire.

"Kitty. Is 'twat' a bad word?" I'd ask.

"'Twat,'" Kitty responded, taking time to exhale her lungful of cigarette smoke, "is a good word."

"How about 'cunt'? Or 'prick'? Or 'shit'?"

"Those are all perfectly good words," Kitty responded. In the end I finally figured out there was only one word Kitty would take time to black out in the bathroom stalls, and that word was "nigger," which explains why her ice didn't exactly break the first time she met my father.

MY PROBLEM, I'M CONSTANTLY TOLD, is that I need to get laid. Which is funny, because I always thought I could trace the bane of my existence to sex. What has it ever led to except a big psycho pit of poisonous expectations? I have no idea how to behave, and I realize I never did. I can think of pathetically few examples in which it all went sort of seamlessly and I got to go on my way without ending up weighted with attachment.

Lary and Grant, I swear, are no help whatsoever. All they ever do is point out my problem (or what they see as my problem anyway) without offering any viable solution. Grant has even offered to *service* me, which isn't as crazy as you might think. He's only been gay for 20 percent of his life, so it'd be nothing for him to cross back into hetero territory to help out a friend, or even just for old-time's sake, not that we ever slept together in the old times.

In fact, in the old times, when Grant was a heterosexual seminary student, he was so busy fucking other women he hardly had time to worry about being gay. The only problem was that, if the women weren't already married, he'd end up marrying them himself, which, in case you haven't noticed, sucks all the fun out of anonymous sex. So even *Grant* has a hard time having meaningless heterosexual sex. I think this is the sole reason he turned gay.

As for me, it's not like I can become a gay man for a day and get all my bestial buffalo-sex needs sated with one visit to the public toilet and then return to my family with nothing more than a mountain of HandiWipes in the backseat to betray me. No, I am totally trapped in my hetero-ness. Plus, I don't even think I *have* bestial buffalo-sex needs.

That right there is pressure, I tell you. For example, Grant must be some kind of super cock rocket when it comes to sex. Of course, this is by his own account, but he's been telling these accounts for years now and I just put it all together.

"Wait, that makes *six guys* in one day," I interjected one afternoon at Java Vino. "Don't you nap?"

Java Vino is a new coffeehouse that Grant likes because, well, it's new, and Grant has probably fucked everybody at all the old ones. Anyway, Grant's been telling me these stories for years now, but it's only recently that I've been listening to them with any intensity. In fact, lately his stories have become my basic reason for living. My favorite is the one about when he was a seminary student and he had a cluster fuck in a communal shower with a preacher and his wife. Just *hearing* that story amounts to the most sex I've had in—Christ, I'm embarrassed to tell you how long it's been.

Lary likes listening to Grant, too. He doesn't even hang up on him anymore like he used to when he realized they were practically having phone sex. Now he puts all pretense aside and just pushes eagerly, "Yeah. Yeah, go on . . ."

I myself don't have any more stories. I told the one about the Danish backpacker on the island of Santorini, and the French Canadian on the ferryboat back to Italy, and whatever other meager, stupid-ass exploits from my college days that pale in comparison.

Once a flight attendant introduced me to her fiancé, a pilot about whom she'd been blathering for the entire three days of our trip, and for two solid years after that I wondered why the hell this man was so rude to me, practically running away before his future wife even finished saying, "This is who I've been telling you about . . . ," and then one day it just hit me like a complete comet from the archives of my repressed memories: oh, my God! I had bestial buffalo sex with that man on a layover in Frankfurt in 1998!

I still like to laugh about that, how he remembered me and I did not remember him. It marks just about the only time I ever had meaningless sex that remained meaningless. I'd use the occasion to encourage myself if not for the fact that it really was forgettable in almost every sense.

Then there was the time I fucked a friend. A dumb move, I admit. He loved me from afar and I toyed with him like he was a trained puppy. When I moved to Atlanta he wrote me from California, revealing his heart like an unhealed wound, all out in the open for the first time and worried what I might think. I never even wrote him back. To this day I believe my own heart is uglier because of that. To this day I am less inclined to reveal it.

"You need to get laid," Lary says again, and all I do is shake my head. That is so not *even* what I need. Either that or it is a fraction, a *molecule*, of what is missing in my life. But my friends, my fucking friends, only know how to offer solutions that would work for them. "I'll fuck you," Grant kindly offers again, which cheers me up a little, but not all the way.

MY CHILD DOES NOT WANT to return to earth. We've been on Mars for about an hour now, a planet that looks a lot like a restaurant on Broadway, complete with costumed characters that intermittently visit our table to give my girl a three-eyed high five, and Milly is ecstatic.

She's at that age where she believes everything. "Mars looks like a cave," she says. And it does. We're in the windowless underbelly of the Paramount Building, and they've fashioned quite a cavelike little paradise down here. Everything is illuminated with a red glow, and everything looks good this way. The food, which is actually only passable theme-park fare, could be covered in *E. coli* and still look edible under this light. I could be a thousand-year-old sea tortoise and still look fuckable under this light. I wish the whole world was under this light.

But it's not, and there's only so long you can sit on Mars before the crap the street vendors sell on Times Square starts calling your name. I coax Milly into leaving by telling her that back in Atlanta we have our very own alien who lives down the street, and she believes me. Good reason, Lary is the least human of anyone I know. So if this is a lie, it's a good lie.

Santa is also a good lie, I believe, so I'm feeding the Santa myth to my kid like it's covered in chocolate and topped with a cherry. I don't care what people think. Earlier I took Milly to the Radio City Christmas Spectacular, where she sat agog at the sight of Santa and his dancing North-Pole population. That's right, I'm hoping she'll glean that the world is a sweet place, with candy-cane lanes and snow flakes aflutter.

On stage behind the Rockettes, there was a backdrop depicting the New York skyline, minus the twin towers, of course. To me it still looked a like a beautiful smile with its two front teeth knocked out, but by the time my girl grows up that gap will have been filled, if not by other buildings then by simple mass mental adjustment to what had transpired. The skyline will no longer be missing something, it will just be what it is, like the armless statue of Venus de Milo, which is so radiant in her flawed state we'd never think to consider her unwhole.

So I let Milly believe in Santa, which she does still, even after seeing a hundred of them dancing on stage in a "Santa Can Be All Places at All Times" kinda number. I'm so glad they performed that. I was wondering how I was gonna explain that part.

Throughout, Milly was wide-eyed with trust. I'll need to keep that mental Polaroid deep within me for the rest of my life, because soon enough the day will come when she'll be a hard sell, not believing in anything, much less a word I say, even if I'm pointing to the ocean and telling her it's wet. That's just the sweet punishment of parenthood: to endure the diminishing level of your usefulness in your children's eyes.

It pains me to remember how young I was myself when skepticism befell me. When I was five, my family lived in a bungalow where we kept the Christmas lights up all year. They were the big-bulbed kind, too, and multicolored, the kind that cremate your corneas if you look at them long enough.

We had a fake Christmas tree that was only about twice as complicated to construct as a Moroccan museum. We kids put that thing together every year, and the result was a crotchety-old-lady-with-osteoporosis kind of Christmas tree, but we packed on enough lights, tinsel, and canned snow to cover up the crooked spots.

One Christmas Eve night my father very excitedly called my sisters and me outside to look at the sky. "Look up there," he shouted. *"It's Santa Claus in the sky on his sleigh."*

"Where? Where?" we shouted. "There! There!" he shouted back. And we kept peering into the sky where he pointed, through the reddish glow of the big-bulbed lights, peering so fiercely until suddenly my sister exclaimed wondrously, "I see him."

"I see him, too."

"Me, too."

And there we three stood, seeing Santa way high in the sky over our front yard, with nothing but my father's word making it real. It was just two years later, at the age of seven, that I stopped believing his word. I don't remember how exactly, I think the belief just dissipated from me like air from a slow leak. One day it was simply all gone, so that when my father pointed to the air on Christmas Eve I no longer saw anything, not even the reddish glow from the big bulbs.

"Do you see him?" My father asked, his face close to mine, his eyes as wide as his smile, his arm straining to point at a spot on the empty horizon.

"You see him, don't you?" he implored, with the hint of fretfulness on the edge of his voice. His wide eyes began rounding in a different way as he looked at me, his silent daughter.

"I see him," I said finally, with forced wonderment. "Yes, he's right there," I lied.

With that my father's face, fueled by my good lie, radiated with delight again, and he continued to point to the empty sky. That is how I remember him, reaching heavenward, where somewhere there was a Santa on his way to a sweet place, with candy-cane lanes and snowflakes aflutter.

LAST NIGHT LARY finally slept with a gay man. Before I go any further I'd like to say that, after all the time I wasted breaking into this man's house looking for evidence he's a big huge homo—and *failing*, I might add—you'd think it'd be harder for him to come right out with it. But no, he came right out with it.

"I slept with Daniel last night," he said, "or I tried to, anyway."

It was five in the morning at the Universal Studios Hilton, and I was downstairs in the lobby reading the last chapters of a crappy paperback, trying to deal with a bad case of jet brain. I swear, fly me anywhere west of Texas and I sleep worse than a cocktail waitress in a cocaine factory. That morning I was downstairs reading because my own hotel room was full of sleeping women—not gay, mind you, but then we can sleep with each other without getting tagged as such.

"You wanna know the worst part about sleeping with gay men?" Lary complained. "It's all that *whispering*,"

Evidently Daniel and Grant had decided to get up in the middle of the night to try on all the clothes they bought at thrift stores the afternoon before. Grant tried on his "man skirt" again, which he thinks is very masculine, as well as his black-and-white polka-dotted faux-fur porkpie hat and his orange upholstered "man bag."

"That looks *great* on you!" "You have *got* to wear that!" Lary could hear those two whispering.

Giant Michael was there, too, in the other bed. Earlier Grant had dictated the sleeping arrangements. "It'll be boy-girl-boy-girl," he insisted, and the hetero contingent didn't argue. They know Grant's motto this week: "Faith over fear, don't choose the wrong f-word."

So, yes, one gay man was relegated to each bed. Grant immediately tagged Giant Michael's bed for himself. Michael is 6 feet 7 inches after all, and tall men are known for packing a python in their pants, not that that's a bad tag to live with.

Anyway, they were all in L.A. to be in the audience on *The Tonight Show* with Jay Leno, but you'd think they thought this was *The Price Is Right* or something, seeing as how they were set to storm the stage in case their name got called. Even Lary got so excited he actually entertained Grant's suggestion he wear a hazard-cone-colored jumpsuit like the kind prisoners wear when they pick up trash on the roadside.

"It's *perfect*," Grant shrieked when Lary tried it on, and I must say I agreed, but Lary decided against it, saying he didn't want to be pigeon-holed as an escaped convict. That surprised me, because I'd have thought he would have loved that tag. I swear, you think you know people.

I remember I tagged my brother-in-law, Eddie, for a loser the second I was sober enough to get a good look at him. That impression lasted for about eight years, roughly, even though he'd been cleaned up and productive for most of that time. He quit smoking, even, and had pretty much done just about everything else to wipe away the last remnants of dirt-clod to reveal the diamond underneath, but when I looked at him I still kept seeing the troubled person I'd tagged him as years ago, whereas my sister never saw that. She always saw the diamond inside.

Before they settled in Dayton, when Eddie had asked her to move with him from her familiar San Diego to the middle of the Arizona desert to build a spiritual retreat, my sister hardly hesitated. He called it Angel Ranch, and he had dreams of people coming in droves to commune with nature and meditate. When I heard their plans I laughed so hard I thought I'd shoot champagne out my nose. "Jesus God, are they gonna fall on their asses or what?" I snorted.

But damn if Eddie didn't build that ranch, a series of rustic cabins surrounding a courtyard, with his bare hands. He dug a manmade pond, powered the entire compound with solar energy, and created a copper-accented sculpture garden on the property. I visited them there on occasion, and at sunset the statues sparkled against the barren desert ground from which they sprang, and if I were a spiritual person I might have meditated, but I was not.

Though a few droves came to commune with nature after all, Eddie's dream didn't last. Those two lost everything, even the Indian blankets on the bunks in the cabins surrounding the courtyard. They had to leave it all behind and drive away with hardly more than what their car could carry, passing under the decorative archway Eddie had carved as a gateway to the property. Eddie didn't look back, but if he did he would have seen the copper-accented sculpture garden shimmering in the distance, glowing like a diamond in a sea of dirt clods, and I think that's when I finally started to take my tag off of him.

But others remain. As of today, though, I will probably stop breaking into Lary's house, and not just because he has finally given me a key, but because I've decided Lary simply is who he is and there's no need to look further. "I can't believe all I had to do to keep from getting tagged," Lary said in the lobby that morning, "was sleep with a gay man."

MEXICO, I BELIEVE, is a bad place to be when you are half dead, and Bill is not even half dead. "I'm all the way dead," he croaks.

He is not in Mexico either, not yet. But he is close. We both are. We're in San Diego. I came here to visit Bill in the hospital, but since, according to Bill, they did what they could to kill him there, he checked his own lymphoma ass out before I got here, and after a bunch of panicked phone calls I found him in a hotel next to a freeway that leads to El Centro. When we used to live here with my mother, my little sister and I once took this freeway to drive to Mexicali, where we boarded a train to Mazatlan and partied like people who had their entire lives before them.

Today Bill has his entire life before him, there just might not be much of it left is all. He looks about as bad as I expected he would, not any worse, which is good. He is not in good spirits, but he'll pretend he is, which is also good, because that means he has resolve. As I'm sure you can tell, I am not new to this.

I am not new to Mexico either. My mother checked into a Mexican cancer clinic as a last resort fourteen years ago, and to this day I can take you straight there. I'm proud of this because, believe me, that place is hard to navigate. You have to cross the border into Tijuana and follow the road signs to Rosarito Beach, but then you break left onto an obscure road that traverses a ravine, at the bottom of which are dozens of rusty mutilated cars with corpses probably decades old still trapped inside, then you take another left onto the second dirt road past the abandoned gateway to a once-ambitious-but-never-built shopping mall, and right there, at the bottom of a cul-de-sac (if you can call it a cul-de-sac, because it's really just a road that ended), is a big mirrored building where, for five hundred dollars a day, Haiti-trained doctors administer alternative cancer treatments not approved in the United States.

That place is full of people full of hope. If they don't have that they might as well save their money and die with their pants around their ankles like Elvis. All except Bill, though, who is hopeless and always has been. Hope is not what keeps him alive. His crusty cantankerousness keeps him alive. His complaining about life keeps him alive.

"I'm all the way dead," he complains again, hugging me but barely, he is so weak. He's lying flat on his back, fully clothed in a freshly made bed. From what I hear he actually paid in advance for this room, whereas he paid the hospital for his thirty-day stay with a check, most likely from some phantom bank in Nicaragua, where he's been living as a fugitive from mediocrity for the last few years.

"You crusty old bucket of barnacles, you've been threatening to die for damn decades. I ain't fallin' for it this time," I tell him, and I think I mean it. Bill probably is not done yet, even though he is on his way to the clinic in Mexico on the road that ended. That place finished my mother, but that's only because it was her last resort. Bill is far from his last resort. He can barely sit up, but his eyes are still clear and blue, even larger now because the rest of him has shrunk. He has no hope, mind you, but he has *plans*.

"In the hospital I bled to death a couple of times," he's telling me in normal tones, as if he were talking about a toilet overflow at the *pensione* he owns with my sister in Granada, "then I had a massive heart attack, which sucked. Those are pretty painful, you know. . . ."

The problem, he continues, is not even the lymphoma. It's his heart, which evidently is too weak to sustain a full blast of chemotherapy. So he is on his way to the Tijuana clinic to strengthen it so he can come back and live through conventional medicine. I suppose I'll go with him, even though nothing scares me more than getting stuck in Mexico with a dead relative, and Bill is not really my relative, even though he's family. He was my mother's best friend when her life was leaving her like air from an old beach ball. He found that mirrored clinic at the end of the Mexican road, and he drove my mother's used VW van down there with me next to him and my mother lying flat on her back in the bed of the van, too weak to sit up. Bill pointed out the landmarks as he went.

"You're gonna need to know this," he said. Mexico is famous for bad roads and bad road signage. I probably still have college friends stuck down there who, over a decade later, have not found their way back. "At the orange trailer you take a left, got that?" Bill continued. "Look for the gravel driveway with the big painted plaster Virgin Mary at the end. . . ."

Thus I memorized the path to the place on the road that ended. Bill was right. I was gonna need to know this.

HONNIE AND TODD SOLD THEIR HOUSE. Or I should say Grant sold their house. It took a showman like Grant to move that property once all the real-estate agents in the neighborhood put the bad juju on it. It's funny that the damn crack house across the street sold in a week, but it took months for Honnie and Todd's house to sell, even though it was all painted and polished with potted plants on the porch and all the smoke damage in the basement relatively repaired.

The drug dealer next door, he is gone, too. He bashed all their windows in again, every single one, all the new windows they had replaced since the last time he bashed them all in. After that, though no one in the immediate vicinity who witnessed the act would file a formal report with the police, there was nonetheless such a show of support for Honnie and Todd by other neighbors that the police actually had to start at least appearing as if they were doing their job, especially since the mayor got involved and held a press conference right in Honnie's living room.

The mayor is a shady son of a bitch himself, about a half a step ahead of being indicted for fraud on all kinds of counts, and let's not forget the big controversy surrounding the Atlanta strip clubs, a number of which were claiming he extorted money from them to keep them in operation only to shut them down anyway. So maybe it's because of this that he decided he needed some image enhancement. Whatever the reason, the mayor picked Honnie and Todd's plight as a platform, and you should have seen that crack dealer's face when the news vans pulled up and parked on his yard.

About a week later his house was raided by vice and

they hauled his drug-dealing, dog-fighting ass off to jail along with his purple spandex-covered hellbitch of a girlfriend. It turns out they were living there on a low-income Section 8 allotment, which means the owner was receiving a government subsidy to supplement their rent. The owner of the house, of course, could not care less that his tenant was terrorizing the neighborhood, but the government is fairly averse to subsidizing drug dealers, or at least small-time drug dealers, and once the owner realized his monthly, taxpayer-funded lunch ticket was in jeopardy, he evicted their mean-hearted, arson asses onto the street.

The drug dealer and his girlfriend had to leave the neighborhood after they made bail, and they could not even wreak any farewell havoc, either, because all their drugs had been confiscated, so they had no product with which to barter collusion from the crack cronies, and without the crack cronies as ready witnesses to falsify police reports, he could no longer tell police he was threatened by anyone. This effectively took his biggest weapon away, which in turn neutralized his lesser weapons. So he left and took his passel of torn-up, dog-fought pit bulls with him.

Honnie's family left next. We begged them to stay. Now that the drug dealer next door was gone, the neighborhood was almost nice. They even caught the cop killer Jamil Al-Amin. They found him hiding in a swamp down in Whitehall, Alabama, so it's not like he's lurking around with his assault rifle anymore, either. He's in jail awaiting a capital murder case claiming, of course, that he was framed as part of a government conspiracy. But Honie and Todd had had enough of Capitol View. They wanted out, and who could blame them.

As soon as the last remnants of the drug dealer's evicted belongings were sifted through and dispersed among the miscreants that remained behind, Honnie put a sign in her yard. Her house was the nicest house for sale in the neighborhood, and it should have sold in a nanosecond, but real-estate agents steered their customers away. Months went by before it fell to Grant to take over.

Grant has twelve hundred titles up his ass: he's a licensed social worker, a notary public, and a minister, among other things, and goddam if he doesn't also have a real-estate license left over from about five hundred lives ago. He had about twelve minutes before that license expired, so he set to work and sold that house for them in a few weeks. He said if he can talk the pants off a straight man, he can talk someone into buying a fine house in a perfectly passable neighborhood now that the crack house and drug dealer are gone.

But he could not talk Honnie and Todd into staying. I hated to see them go. I really did. They had a yard sale soon beforehand, and I bought their vintage dinette set even though it would never fit into the tiny butler hutch I have for a dining room. They needed the money, though. Lord knows it's expensive to put out fires and repair windows every five minutes. It's expensive to be the examples the drug dealers are trying to set for what the rest of us in the neighborhood can expect if we try to resist them. It's expensive to resist them anyway and fight for your right to live peacefully in your own home.

"It has taken its toll, believe me," says Honnie. She handed me her brand new messenger bag I just bought for ten dollars, and it wasn't until I got home I realized she had put inside it a dress of hers she had for sale, which I'd admired but couldn't afford. I wish I had known she'd done that so I could have thanked her before she left. In fact, I wish I could have thanked her period. I wish we all could have thanked her and her family both.

OUR CHRISTMAS TREE IS NAKED from the waist down, which really shatters my confidence. It's not that I care what the neighbors think, because all they see shining in our window is the tree's glorious upper half, festooned in all our *outdoor* lights, no less. Grant insisted on that. No anemic little pin lights for him, because pin lights are for pussies. So our tree has lights as big as tortoise eggs, and bright enough to bleach your irises unless you squint. In fact, I'd advise against looking directly at our tree's upper half at all unless it's through a shaded windshield.

But the lower half, now that's a different story. It started out decorated like the rest, but then we unleashed Milly, who took five minutes to pilfer every ornament she could reach. The ones I didn't pull out of her mouth I pulled out from under her covers. They made a pretty pile in the middle of her mattress, all the colorful bulbs, like the hidden booty of a baby pirate. I can't believe I almost let her keep them. I really did, but then I thought, what if they break? That would look pretty bad, right? My daughter sleeping on a bed of shattered glass.

We can't have that. Think how it would look, me allowing my child to nap on a nest of broken ornaments. We can't be busting me as a crappy mom in front of everybody like that. So I swept all the ornaments out of her reach, and as a consequence Milly shrieked so piercingly that lobsters in the middle of the ocean were probably signaled by her sound waves, but at least for the next five seconds or so I was certain I was exuding the appearance of a protective mother. At least there's that, right? I mean, appearances are important.

Just ask the fake charity worker who collects money through car windows on a street corner near our house. She thrusts a white bucket with a bogus aid-organization logo on it through your window, and she's figured out that if she appears to have a handicap, people can be a lot more forthcoming with the fork-outs. I've noticed that over the past few months she's perfected an entire fake sign language, one she supplements by moving her lips in an exaggerated way without making any actual noise. So people assume she's deaf and dole out the green. I never give her any money myself because I've seen her walk straight to the crack house with her bucket of coins, turning to wave at people who *call her name*, but other than that her new act is impressive.

There is another guy in our neighborhood who begs door to door, claiming he's a veteran who needs milk for his newborn. That's a double whammy, and I guess he figures he needs a double whammy in this neighborhood because we are not exactly a bunch of PTA parents here. I myself never trusted this man because newborns don't drink cow's milk, but Lary—crusty Lary, who once roared at me for fifteen solid minutes because I gave a handout to a homeless man in exchange for a free newspaper—helped him out anyway. A few days later he saw the same man loitering in front of the crack house around the corner, and the man tried to explain his presence there by saying he was ministering to sinners, but from Lary's point of view the man didn't appear to be ministering, he appeared to be participating, and Lary told him if he ever knocked on our doors again he would rip his heart out through his rib cage.

Thus hardened, I've been confining my acts of goodwill to cutting small checks to big corporate charities lately—except for the occasional bag of pecans the neighborhood boys sell. I hate pecans, but I usually buy a bag anyway because it reminds me of when I was a kid and had to sell cupcakes door to door to earn money. I remember a fat lady named Mrs. Freedle who lived up the street from us and who always bought half a tray. Always. That was a slam dunk fortune for us, and she'd let us hang out and pet all her cats, too, who were really fat as well. We used to laugh about it afterward, like how we could always count on her to cough over the money on account of her cravings for sweets.

But one day we knocked on her door and her grown daughter answered and told us Mrs. Freedle was in the hospital due to her really bad diabetes, which is a disease that prohibited her from eating sugar, she told us. So it turned out Mrs. Freedle never even ate our cupcakes after all, she was just buying them to promote our enterprise. After that I regretted having judged her by her appearance, figuring she was feasting on our cupcakes when really she was feeding them to her cats. When she came back from the hospital, she still paid for the cupcakes but insisted we give them away to someone who appeared to be hungry. So I always think of her when I pay the boys for a bag of pecans. "Give them to someone who looks hungry," I say.

GRANT STILL SAYS I SHOULD fuck a fat black man. Today, for some reason, Grant once again thinks fucking a fat black man will solve everyone's woes, and I didn't even know I had woes. I thought I had everything kind of quasi-handled, so why would I need a man in my life?

"I didn't say you need a man in your life," says Grant, "I said you need a man in *you*."

It's the day after Grant's 109th birthday, or so he says, and he thinks that makes him sage enough to dole out guidance. "You're a fine one to give advice," I tell him. "You've been gay for six entire years and last weekend was your first appearance at Gay Pride."

I've even been to Gay Pride more often than Grant. Trapped in my heteroness, Gay Pride is like a droolfest for me with all its beautiful men, all these awesome physical morsels dancing about like chew toys on the end of a string. I usually go with Daniel and his brother Darell, who has recently gotten himself immensely buff—even his head is more muscular now. Leave it to a gay man to figure out how to improve muscle definition in his *fore-head*. Maybe it's all that oral sex.

Daniel's boyfriend Mitch has nicknamed Darell "Slut," and Darell doesn't seem to mind. I wish everyone was that unfazed by the word. When I was thirteen, I hung out for a time with a genuine slut named Mary, who had an extra-long thumbnail she said she could use to steal extra cocaine when the mirror was passed to her. I didn't understand what she was talking about, so she illustrated by bringing the inside of her thumbnail to her nos-

tril and sniffing mightily. I still didn't understand, but pretended
I did.

Mary lived a few blocks away from me, and before my friends
and I got to know her we knew *of* her. Everybody did. She was
pleasant but sloppy looking, with a very developed body for a
fourteen-year-old. She could have passed for eighteen, which evidently she did, because my father knew her from the neighborhood bar where he spent his days. My father told us that she
picked up men at the bar and had sex with them in their cars in the
parking lot.

"She's a slut," he'd say. Why my father expressed contempt,
rather than concern, for a fourteen-year-old girl who fucked his
friends in the parking lot of a bar escapes me.

Later, after my friends and I got to know Mary, she introduced
me to Marlboro 100s (as opposed to the Marlboro regulars I'd been
stealing from my father since I was nine) and Neil Young music.
She was the first girl I met who was passionate about a particular
music even though the singer, as she put it, "is so fucking ugly." Up
until that point I don't think I knew ugly people could be talented.

Mary normally acted very self-assured and knowledgeable,
but she was only fourteen after all, and we were even younger than
her, so it was only a matter of time until her youth reared itself, her
toughness wore off, and she began to goof around. Once, Mary
peddled me around town on the handlebars of my bicycle. She
wore a safari hat and I waved a tennis racket in the air, and we sang
"Old MacDonald" at the top of our lungs. It was testimony to our
immaturity that we thought this was the most fun to be had this
side of piloting your own Apollo moon buggy, and we laughed so
hard we almost turned our tonsils inside out.

As we rode toward my house, I asked Mary to slow down because I needed to use the bathroom. She asked to come inside,
and, though it was the middle of the day and my father should
have been at the bar, I could nonetheless see his car in the driveway, which meant he was home instead. I had to tell Mary she

wasn't allowed in my house, and asked her to wait for me outside on the sidewalk. "My father says you're a slut," I told her.

For some reason I didn't think she'd be hurt by that, I thought she'd think it was cool. But Mary was very hurt by it; there was nothing I could say to make her feel better. She wouldn't wait for me, and stormed away, confused and tearful.

She never spoke to me again, but years later I heard she got herself a girlfriend. "Who would've thought that trashy Mary was really a lesbian?" laughed some of the codgers who hung out at the bar with my father. Today, when I go to Gay Pride, I see a lot of women who could be her, and they seem happy. But to this day I feel sorry for what I said to my slut friend Mary, and especially ashamed for asking her to wait for me outside.

CALL ME A PUSSY, but dead children freak me out. First there was the one who was eighteen and I guess you can argue he wasn't a child, but eighteen is pretty damn young to be beaten to death with a flashlight.

And I guess you can argue, as many did, that he really wasn't beaten to death with a flashlight. Many argue that he would have died anyway, without the beating, on account of the drugs in his system, but I am of the mind that the beating didn't help at all.

And so were a lot of my neighbors, who gathered together and set fire to the house a few doors down from mine, as setting fire to people's houses seems to be the neighborly way of settling disputes in my neighborhood. The house was owned by the man blamed for the boy's death. He is not the man who gave the boy the drugs or even the person who beat him with a flashlight, but he is the man who called the police when the boy was trespassing on his property. The police in turn chased the boy, tackled him, and then the said beating commenced. Coincidentally or not, the boy died right after that.

So I guess you could argue, as many did, that that dead kid doesn't count, but that was my first dead kid and my first burned-down house since I'd moved into Capitol View a few months prior, so I personally counted him.

Then there was the next boy, who was in his early teens and you cannot possibly argue that he wasn't a kid. He was shot and killed by yet another kid for cheating at dice. This happened right across the street from the house that burned, and should not be confused with the incident in which a two-year-old was shot in the parking lot of an apartment complex nearby. That bullet passed through that girl's leg and killed her grandmother, who was holding her at the time. The girl and her grandmother were unintended targets (someone cheating at dice was the target) whereas in the cheating-at-dice case that happened a few doors down from mine, that target was reached.

There would be more burned houses and more dead children, like the teenager who was killed twelve days after my own child was born, shot at a MARTA stop by, police speculated, a jealous boyfriend. And let's not forget the twelve-year-old who was shot in the chest that Halloween for throwing eggs in Phoenix Park, which was more in Lary's neighborhood than mine, but Lary lives just three minutes away from me. Lary, though, is not all that freaked out by dead children, even that newborn that was found in a driveway up the way from him. Someone had bashed its head in, tied it up in a plastic sack, and tossed it onto a driveway.

"All I know is I didn't have anything to do with it," Lary swore.

He had come to my place to give me tips on how to bullet-proof Milly's room, a precaution I was starting to suspect would not matter. First, all I had in terms of materials were cookie sheets and cake pans, and Lary said they were not strong enough to stop a bullet, "but it would probably slow it down," he said in a manner as close to comfortingly as his crusty barnacle ass could muster. But then he had to ruin that, even, by telling me a bullet doesn't need a window to get inside.

"It could pass right through the wall," he insisted. "Especially this wall," he added, knocking on the new drywall that enclosed the former porch that now made up the nursery. So at that we went outside to assess any possible trajectories, especially from Crack Corner at the north end of the street, which is where a preponderance of the shootings had occurred. In the end we determined that the safest place for her bed was in front of the bureau right next to my own bed. That way, if a bullet passed through the wall to reach her it would also have to pass through my underwear drawer as well, which contained a bunch of bras with so much padding that a skydiver with a faulty parachute could land on them and live. There, I thought, it's the best I could do.

But then I thought again. I read that the mother whose son was killed in the park near Lary had heard the shot the instant it happened. She ran to her son and reached him in time to hold his hand as he died. I'm sure she did the best she could have in the years that led up to that point, and I'm sure she tried hard to change whatever circumstances left her to live with her child in a place where kids were commonly killed; those changes just didn't happen fast enough is all.

So I put the cake pans in the windows and was mindful of trajectory patterns from the corner where the other kids had been killed, but I also kept thinking about the mother who held her boy's hand as he died, and how her changes didn't happen fast enough. So I decided to start making some changes of my own, starting with a new mortgage lender, and you'd be surprised at how quick you can be when you're trying to outrun a bullet on its way to an unintended target.

'M CURLED UP UNDER MY DESK AGAIN; snarly-haired, gibbering, swatting at imaginary insects. I don't even know what's wrong. Maybe it's about my job, for which I wear a uniform. I wear a uniform and a nametag and an apron. Sometimes I'm self-conscious about that. Sometimes I wonder if I'll always be an apron-wearing, nametag-sporting bovine with hands all rough from lugging stuff. And then to make it worse I'll get out my mental crystal ball and see myself at sixty, upper arms flapping like two turkey wattles, a face like a frying pan, and the nametag still there, the *apron* still there, setting quite a nice example for my daughter.

Jesus God, just ignore me. I'll get over it. I'm operating at optimum stress capacity is all. I just put another house under contract, with a seemingly elephantine mortgage, and I'm petrified, but I've got Milly to think about. I didn't go through this when I bought the house I presently occupy, because I paid maybe twenty dollars for this place. I remember thinking I could afford the mortgage even if I became confined to a wheelchair with a body like a ball of melted wax, working the controls with my tongue. What do I have to lose? I thought, and signed the papers.

Right beforehand I remember I'd gone to the New Orleans Jazz Festival, where I had occasion to dance on stage in my underwear and hang out for a time with two young heroin addicts, Ryan and Billy, who were on the faltering road to recovery. Ryan had been my waiter one morning and then greeted me later that day on the street, walking his bicycle beside me. "You're alone again," he said. "We'll fix that."

Soon we arrived at the place of his friend Billy, who had tattooed eyelids and was in the process of getting thrown out of his apartment. As we waited outside for Billy to gather his things, Ryan showed me the track marks on his arms, which were faint because it had been nine months since he'd shot up. "What drugs do you do?" he asked.

"None," I replied.

"Lucky you," he said, and meant it.

Billy emerged and was very gracious. "I'm sorry you have to see me like this," he said, "but it's very nice to meet you." Everything he owned fit on the seat of his bike, which he walked beside Ryan and I. Billy had just been evicted at gunpoint because his roommate caught him with drugs in the apartment. "Did you do the drugs?" Ryan asked him.

"No, I was just *thinking* about doing them!" answered Billy, grief in his voice. "He doesn't know what it's like," he said of his former roommate. "I'm a hooked fish, he's not a hooked fish. *He has no idea what it's like!*"

"I know what it's like," Ryan comforted his friend. Ryan could relate, he knew what it felt like to have one thing—in their case this drug—be the source of both boundless rapture and unendurable pain. He knew the delicious anguish it was to be the slave of such a thing. "I'm a hooked fish, too."

"Hooked fish," Billy repeated softly, shaking his head. "Is she a hooked fish?" he asked, indicating me.

"She's a free fish," Ryan said. Then we reached their destination, a tiny bar that was packed with revealers in the early afternoon. Ryan and Billy went inside, but after hearty goodbyes I decided to continue on alone. Free fish, I thought as I walked along. Free fish, that be me.

That seems like a million years ago, when actually it's been barely an eye blink. Now here I am, everything I swore I'd never be. For example, I said I'd never complain about getting older, but it's hard to be a hundred years old and not talk about it. Not that I'm exactly a hundred, but it feels that way when you go to places like Disney World and see thousands of parents pushing their perfectly healthy adolescent children around in rented plastic rickshaws and you hear yourself say, "When I was a kid I had to walk with my own feet!" Seriously, if I ever asked my parents to wheel me around all day like a lazy little pope they'd have coughed up ten years worth of tar and nicotine, they'd be laughing so hard. I mean, we grew feet for a reason, right? Or are we in the process of devolving back into the blobs we once were? What is the world coming to, with Disney World packed with little imposter invalids? Is this any place to raise children?

There it is again, me being what I swore I wouldn't: someone freaked about the future. It wasn't that long ago that I couldn't see any further into the future than my minimart burrito, which the microwave finishes cooking in about four minutes. I was happily selfish and completely tunnel-visioned, running through the rain with arms outstretched. I could not have cared less, for example, about the danger of croaking like a lab rat from a mosquito-borne disease like the West Nile virus. Back then I would have glided naked on a skateboard through a festering nest of teeming mosquito larvae if it meant a decent margarita on the other side.

But not today. Not after this comet called momhood, which is just one sack of surprises after another, isn't it? For example, Daniel points out that I've bought eight cans of Cutter insect repellant this summer, which he says is excessive. But I'm thinking about the *future*, see? And what I envision is cans of Cutter everywhere, at least two within arm's reach of any possible position in our household, so I won't even *think* of walking outside without coating my baby like a little cob of corn. I bought two more cans yesterday, I figure I can use them to physically club each mosquito as well. You can never be too careful.

You can never be too careful? I certainly didn't inherit that from my mother, who once broke her foot hang gliding in Mexico and didn't figure it out for five days. She also once fought off a biker with a broken Hurricane glass in New Orleans (okay, she just brandished it at him as he rode by, but *still*), and when I was seven she sent me almost every day to buy her cigarettes from the child molester who owned the liquor store next to my father's favorite bar (when she found out he was a pervert she took her business elsewhere, but *still*).

So you see? I should have grown up daring, with wild hair and arms outstretched every chance I got. I shouldn't be sitting here right now, a hundred-year-old person who is not a hundred years old. I thought I'd at least be tragic by this time in my life. The object of cult fame. Some kind of female Bukowski living under a freeway overpass creating masterpieces scratched out on fast-food wrappers and old grocery sacks. Beholden to nothing but embracing everything.

But no. Instead I am enslaved. I am such a big, proud, foolish jar of gibbering mom flesh here under my desk with colorless lips and ragged fingertips, no longer the person with nothing to lose, no longer the loser of nothing. I can hear Milly in the connecting room, making her toddler noises. "I'm a tiger," she trills. "I'm a lion. I'm a kitty cat."

I perk up. She's naming all the members of the feline species, isn't she? Is she a *genius* or what? I emerge from my dark place right then to find her growling at me sweetly with her fingers curled like little paws. The sight of her sends me awash in a roiling ocean of adoration. To think I almost missed out on motherhood, because I had nothing to lose and liked it that way, but now everything, *everything*, teeters on the tiniest strand of hair on Milly's head. Her precious, unbearably vulnerable little vanilla-scented head. God! This is agonizing! I almost want to crawl back under my desk, but instead I kneel down to embrace my girl, who thankfully tolerates it for a good while. Still, long after she wrestles free, I remain there bowed before her, a hooked fish.

HEN I WAS FIVE I used to fantasize about fainting into the arms of another man, preferably during a dangerous battle of some kind. I don't know what that says about me, but there it is; I thought the ultimate was to flat out faint in the middle of everything and be carried away from danger like a burdensome sack of maggots.

I based this on about seven hundred sci-fi movies from the fifties and sixties I watched in which exactly that happened; the female character was always fainting into the arms of the male character, who then somehow had to whisk her to safety *while at the same time* fighting the space monster with an old-time TV for a head.

So my sister and I would practice. We'd feign rushing somewhere only to be confronted by the sight of something so odious our only recourse would be to gingerly place the back of our hands to our foreheads and then collapse into a dainty pile right there on the indoor-outdoor carpeting. There we'd lie with our eyes closed, hissing at each other, "You be the man!" "No, you!"

Nobody wanted to be the man. We both just wanted to be saved.

Eventually we just got ourselves up. "Ain't nobody coming to save you," Lucinda called from the kitchen. Lucinda was the third childcare provider my mother had hired that year. The first one, Mrs. Perry, had to leave us to care for her husband, a trash man who eventually died from an infected sore of some kind. The second lasted for as long as it took her to knock on the door and hear our dog, Echo, barking. By the time my mother answered, the lady was already halfway back to her car. "I don't like dogs," she yelled over her shoulder.

Then came Lucinda, who had four kids of her own. She brought them with her to our house when she was on duty, from her nineteen-year-old daughter to her seven-year-old son, Lucas, including all their friends.

That's how I figured out boys don't fantasize about saving women. They fantasize about saving each other. Lucas and his friends would enact big battle scenes in which they performed feats of bravery to be recounted with awe by their buddies. They were *wounded* in these fantasies, like they'd been shot in the shoulder or something, yet still they were carrying their comrades away from danger. There was much yelling and sweating and gritting of teeth, and in the end they would all kind of collapse into a heap on the safe side of everything. Then they'd tend to each other, lauding the actions of their heroes, until it was time to pack on the imaginary ammunition again.

They were all very brave, I thought. Later Lucinda got fired because she left us in the care of her teenage daughter one day, whose idea of babysitting was to lock us out on the porch while she stayed inside and balled her boyfriend. My mother found out because the neighbors had heard us begging to be let back inside all afternoon. I was kind of sorry to see Lucinda go. I liked being surrounded by brave boys who saved each other.

"Ain't nobody coming to save you," Lucinda had said, and she was right. So I started having fantasies of a different kind. I was going to wake up every morning and conquer things, fell demons. I was going to be *all kinds* of crap. I made a list. I was going to hunt lions on safari in Africa. I was going to build mud huts in Borneo. I was going to become a war correspondent. I was going to traverse the Amazon in a cargo liner.

But I wasn't even that old before reality hit me in the face like a frozen mackerel. First, my grade-school teachers wouldn't even let me wear pants to school, and a lion hunter looks pretty lame in a skirt. Then there was the other basic, everyday drippings of sorrow and disappointment that clung to the walls of my household like moss. My father soon lost his job, then we lost that house and had to move like migrant workers over the next decade, hardly ever staying long enough to fully unpack. In high school I got so tired of walking into classrooms full of strange faces in the middle of the school year that I simply tied up like an overexercised showhorse one day and I wouldn't do it anymore. Then I stopped going to high school all together, and wasn't missed.

I got myself a boyfriend, that handsome heroine addict named Scott, and a job at a cocktail lounge where they didn't blink when I told them I was twenty-three.

From there I made just about every wrong turn you can imagine making, and I felt the fire in me start to die like a treasured pet abandoned on a desert highway. In the end, I did not hunt lions in Africa, I did not build mud huts in Borneo, and I did not traverse the Amazon in a cargo liner. But, hey, I'm here. Ain't nobody come to save me, and still I am here with a whole new definition for bravery. Bravery is the soft voice inside you that won't die, the voice that whispers in your ear each morning and says, "All right, let's try this again."

GIANT MICHAEL SAYS his friend can't go to strip clubs anymore because he keeps falling in love with the dancers. "He wants to bring them home and take care of them," Michael tells me, and I know how his friend feels, because who wouldn't feel sorry for a girl who has to shave her pubic hair into a Hitler mustache to make a living? That has got to suck so bad that your heart just goes out to her.

"I'm sorry," I say to Michael, who has talked me into going to the Cheetah in the middle of the day, "I can't get past the Hitler mustache. It just seems so half done, why don't they just shave it *all* off?"

Michael says something about how it makes for a good signal indicator, like a landing strip, and he thinks it's sexy. But to me it just looks like a caterpillar trying to crawl up the girl's tummy, and that just can't be comfortable. Michael has lured me here, after three years of browbeating, to prove to me that the Cheetah is a nice place after all, especially at this time of the day, when the slobbery happy-hour hogs are off somewhere still hammering away on the keyboards in their cubicles. Michael's right, it's not bad here, I'm not uncomfortable in a room full of naked women, it's just that I think, as a matter of protocol, *men* should be uncomfortable in such a situation, you know? Of course they're not. They act like it's as average as concrete, to be the minority among a crowd of beautiful nude girls.

It doesn't help that the girls are all so damn *nice*. Believe me, bitches don't end up like this for a living; naked and shaking their overcropped poontangs in strangers' faces. Bitches end up married for a living, then their husbands have to come to the Cheetah to be treated nice.

Anyway, even a nice stripper would become a bitch if she had to be married for a living, because sometimes spouses just have a way of sucking all the sweetness out of each other.

Michael is not married, but he was once. So was I, and Michael likes to tell me that since I am now a single mother, I am about as attractive as a bad case of psoriasis. "Seriously, if I didn't know you and I sidled up to you at the bar and started talking to you, the second you mentioned your kid I'd be across the room."

I look at him like he's speaking a different language. "You really think it *matters* to me whether you consider me fuck worthy?" I laugh, and I *must* laugh, because the alternatives are too lame. But really, do some guys seriously think I shouldn't still be ecstatic over my child just because it might mean I'll get laid less from now on? "Christ, Michael, all you're saying is that my kid is an excellent tool for filtering assholes from my life, which is fine with me."

But Michael likes to try and freak me out, anyway. Take the time we realized we both had had the same vivid dream when we were teenagers about a prophet who fell from a spaceship. Michael tried to get me thinking we needed to start a cult, to find all the other people with the same "vision," but I wasn't interested because I knew Michael would get to be the head of the cult (he's 6 feet 7 inches and people tend to do what he says) while I'd have been relegated to single-mom pudding maker and Nike polisher, probably.

Even Michael admits he's kind of a troglodyte in that area. Don't get him wrong; single women are fine—single mothers, though, ought to have an island of their own. I'm reminded of my colleagues when I worked as a copy editor for a city magazine. I remember a fight we had one month when they insisted on giving a person featured in an article, who was a woman and a lawyer, the title of "female attorney."

"I don't believe this," I shrieked. "We don't call the other attorneys 'male attorneys' or 'hermaphro-fucking-dite attorneys' or *whatever*, why do we qualify just the women?" But my ancient coworkers did nothing but light their fiftieth cigarette of the day and die a little more right before my eyes, and who can keep fighting in the face of that?

So I left and here I am today, hanging out at the Cheetah with Giant Michael, my friend the mental simian, who is trying to explain to me that fake boobs are bad but pubic hair shaved into a tiny topiary is just fine. "Don't you think some of these women have children?" I ask, indicating the nude beauties.

"No," he says, "they all take their money home to abusive boyfriends who spend it on drugs."

"Maybe not all," I argue, and I make him give me lots of money to tip the undulating thing on stage. As I give her the money I tell her, "Please take care of yourself."

"Oh, my, God," Michael barks at me when I get back to my seat. "You are such a *mother*."

LARY HAS OFFERED to let me live in his truck, but it doesn't even have a front seat—just a lawn chair perched on the bare metal frame—so I declined. "If I have to I'll move into that decayed crypt you call your home," I tell him instead, "and I plan to use up all your faggy hair-care products while I'm there, too."

Lary, whose clothes are always covered with a Rorschach pattern of stains, nevertheless maintains a meticulous supply of salon-quality hair conditioner in his bathroom, which has proven to be a perk whenever I've had occasion to crash at his place in the past decade. These occasions are usually due to my intermittent bouts of homelessness over the years, and Lary is certain I'm due for another, and I'm worried he's right. You see, I just bought another house, this one in a safer neighborhood, and considering the level of poverty at which a home-buying event traditionally leaves you, nothing makes you feel more in danger of becoming homeless than buying a house.

Or at least I *think* I bought a house last Friday, I'm not sure. I mean, I showed up at closing, with every cent sucked out of my life and into a cashier's check for the down payment, and this check was taken from me, and papers were signed, and keys were exchanged and backs were clapped and documents were filed and I was penniless and felt ready to vomit when it was all done. That part is clear.

What isn't so clear is the actual address of the house I bought. The closing documents don't all agree on that, and I would think the actual address would be an important detail. But what do I know? I'm just the person with the money, and at closing my job was to hand that money out to everyone like a retarded kid who took his father's wallet to the playground.

Later, when I called the attorney's office to point out that the property's address had been misprinted on most of the documents in the closing package, she offered to rerecord the tax information, "if that's what you want." In all, everyone who walked out of the closing office with any money in their pocket is pretty certain the address gaffe is no big deal.

Me? I can't sleep. First of all, I'm really, really poor now. So it's not like I can afford another place when the city forecloses on this one. Not that I wouldn't have paid my taxes, mind you, it's just that I'll have paid them toward a phantom address and not the actual real one for which I hold a key right now. I realize the post-closing person said she'd rerecord that stuff, and she probably will as soon as she has a moment between taking money from people, but I have a sinking feeling that there the only person who ranks lower than a homebuyer is a former homebuyer who has already forked over their check. Think of a college coed who balls a frat boy at a keg party and later still wants him to notice to her; that is the level of success I felt I was having.

"What's that sound?" the post-closing agent probably asked herself when I told her it might be nice if the deed and stuff reflected the correct address as well, "Am I hearing voices from the dead planet of people who have already paid?"

Lary is hardly any comfort. He has the same aversion to bureaucracy that I have, the same certainty that the government fucks up everything bad enough even when all the forms are filled out correctly. So Lary believes I'll accidentally end up in some sewage-pipe of a prison somewhere, or at the very least on his doorstep again, this time with my toddler in tow. I myself don't relish the prospect of childproofing the place known as Lary's House of Broken Glass and Misplaced Narcotics, but at least those salon products can serve to extinguish an inferno if need be. "Really, the truck is very comfortable," he keeps trying to persuade me, "and I'll let you use my garden hose to wash your hair."

Lary himself didn't pay taxes for years before a conscientious ex-girlfriend convinced him to turn himself in before the government found out and had him assassinated. After that an IRS auditor paid him a visit to inventory all his possessions for seizure in case an auction was in order. But the auditor made one tour around the abandoned warehouse Lary calls home, complete with insect larvae, rusty auto-body skeletons, and a tribe of alley cats living on the carport, and quickly discerned that Lary was indigent. "Give us a hundred bucks and we'll call it even," said the auditor, or something like that.

"Easiest escape I ever made," Lary likes to brag. I, on the other hand, believe he still owes a debt to society. He should do community service or something. Yes, that's it, he should house a homeless family. "Now, before I get there, you know that scaffolding you have behind your couch that holds up the roof?" I tell him. "That has got to go."

THIS MUST BE the season for dead stepfathers, I'm thinking, though Grant reminds me that his was real and mine might not have been. "I bet Bill really did marry my mother," I contest. Bill had always said he did, anyway, and he always does what he says. In most cases it takes him a long time to get around to it, but he does it. That's why I should have known he'd die. He always does what he says.

He always said he loved my mother, while she never said anything. But that was her nature. For example, before she died she'd had a quiet affair with her boss that lasted five years. I like to believe he loved her immensely and would have married her in half a heartbeat, but it was not in her nature to marry someone who would love her like that. It was more in her nature to marry someone who loved her like Bill.

"But he lives in his car!" I reminded her one day.

"Not for long. I'm getting a place," Bill said, because he was right there beside her. He was always right there beside her.

And he did what he said, he got a place—an ocean-front apartment with two bedrooms and a balcony overlooking the sand. We still wonder how the hell he pulled that off on the income he made selling, for example, inflatable beach toys (with punctures patched) at the swap meet. He had a roommate, too, a tall, twenty-five-year-old, curly haired god named Brad who was as dumb as a bag of bait. Bill once caught him trying to blow-dry his hair in the bathtub.

Brad would lug things, and my mother and Bill would haggle with people over those things and somehow it paid for their way through life, and then some. My mother rented her own almost-ocean-front apartment not far from Bill's, and about midway between their places they opened their second shop, which sold the higher-end items that came from their warehouse-sized shop in Normal Heights, things like tea cups and crap I couldn't understand. Bill would show me a signet on the bottom of a plate and insist that meant it was worth a lot, and I would wonder why he wasn't selling black lacquer and chrome like the futon store across the street. Bill said he could sell the cup for a fortune, and he did what he said. In short, everything was going so well. Then the dying began.

My mother was first. She had been diagnosed with liver cancer and battled it heroically for a year before she died in her own bed with Bill standing beside her. It was the first time I'd ever seen his big eyes cry. Brad was next, felled by Kaposi's sarcoma brought on by AIDS. Bill insisted the doctors misdiagnosed his friend, adamant that what Brad really suffered from was cat scratch fever. Still, Brad died in bed at the hospital with Bill standing beside him. Then a bunch more of Bill's friends died from other diseases, Bill always beside them. It was the dying, Bill surmised to me later, that made him decide to sell everything and move to Central America.

Not that he hadn't been saying he'd move there since I met him, but I was still surprised when he did it, seeing as how his own health was hardly fabulous. For one, fat blue veins traversed his left leg entirely, making it look like the topography map of a forested region. That can't be good, I thought to myself on a trip out there to see him. But Bill had been threatening to die for centuries, I thought, and this was no different.

The last time I saw him he was in a roadside hotel in San Diego, aiming for Mexico, having abandoned the hospital and the cancer treatment he'd returned to the States to receive. "They want to kill me in there," he insisted, which would have sounded paranoid if not for the fact that this was Bill, and wanting to kill him is a perfectly natural reaction to his presence. His plan was to go to Mexico, where mystical cures awaited.

Grant says all his stepfathers married his mother in real weddings, with pictures and everything. His first stepfather is simply referred to as "the manly influence," because he was a Marine and Grant's mother felt her young sons needed a masculine presence in their lives, especially Grant, who by that time was probably already comparing upholstery swatches to wallpaper patterns. When Grant's mother divorced his first stepfather, the suit didn't go very well in her favor, and she and her three sons jumped on him right there in the courtroom, though Grant said he was just trying to break up the fight. Years later that same judge would preside over Grant's first divorce, and Grant always felt he'd been unjustly scrutinized because of the incident.

His second stepfather, the one Grant always referred to as "Leather Smeller," is the one who died last week. He got his name because his mother found him in the closet one day, Grant recalled, wallowing in her leather coats, smelling her boots and masturbating. *"That's* why she left him?" I marveled, because to me that is not a good reason to leave a perfectly good husband who buys you lots of leather products. If it were me I would have just got in there with him and told him to make room. But Grant's mother is different from me, and their marriage ended, though their friendship never did. At the time Leather Smeller died he was in the hospital, holding the hands of Grant's mother and Grant's third and most recent stepfather. The three of them had been laughing and joking just moments before, relieved that he seemed to have just made it through a rough patch in his illness, when suddenly he grabbed their hands and simply perished right then and there.

"Well, goddam," I said to Grant, "is that a sweet way to die or what?"

"Yes," Grant agreed. He was on his way up there, but not to rummage through Leather Smeller's things as his mother suggested he do, and especially not to retrieve Leather Smeller's brand new laptop his mother insisted he check out, and especially

especially not to haul all Leather Smeller's vintage furniture off to his own storage compartment. Of course he might do all those things anyway, but that's not his reason for going up there. "The man was my stepfather," Grant reminded me. "You'd do the same."

He's probably right. I certainly would have gone to California to find Bill's body out in the desert and made sure it was buried or sprinkled or ground up and fed to pigeons or whatever the hell he wanted if I could have, but Bill went and died and didn't tell anyone where he was headed when it happened. It wasn't until last week I learned that he didn't die in a random hospital, as I'd logically assumed, seeing as how cancer had consumed his body like kudzu. No, Bill died on Christmas damn day in a *casino*, and not just any casino, but one of those big blow-ass casinos that look like an electric oasis in the middle of the California desert. He was laughing and tipping people like a lottery winner, I was told.

"That bastard," I laughed. "I was all worried he died alone clutching his catheter or something."

"Hell no," my sister informed me. "He was on a winning streak. He was throwing money around like it was confetti."

I have to smile at that. Bill always did love to gamble, and like I said he always bet big. He and my mother were junket junkies, always hopping on a bus full of other couples with coupons in their fists to make the eight-hour drive to Vegas and stay for two days nearly free in some subquality hotel, such as the Gold Spike, which is located off the Strip (*off* off the Strip) and has penny poker machines on the wall and blood stains on the carpet. They'd return with big stories about what they won or almost won, or how a blackjack dealer ever so subtly ensured the cards fell in their favor, or how Bill put all his chips on the come line and my mother took them back off right before the dice came up craps, or whatever.

So I guess Bill had checked himself out of the hospital and wasn't headed to a Mexican clinic for unconventional cancer treatment after all. I guess he had his own treatment in mind. I guess he didn't want to gamble his last days on a fight he figured he couldn't win, so instead he headed for his idea of heaven on earth and went out a winner. I think about that and I have to ask—well, goddam—is that a sweet way to die or what? Though still sometimes I worry that Bill died alone, after he himself held the hand of so many friends in their last moments. But then I think maybe he was not alone, maybe they were all there, my mother among them. Maybe they all came to the California desert that Christmas day to gently take Bill by the hand so he could finally close his eyes and, for the last time, do what he always said he would.

S **OMEBODY STOP ME.** Lary sure as hell won't. He's here right now, *encouraging* me. "There should be real flames shooting out right here," he says, indicating the nostrils of the giant Styrofoam dragon standing in my living room, "or at least real smoke. And over here," he continues, moving toward the towering pink and purple castle I personally built, with bricks and everything, "There's got to be a drawbridge, or at least a moat."

Christ, for a second I was actually considering the moat option, thinking maybe I could put the castle in the middle of Milly's inflatable wading pool. That's where I put the palm tree last year, with the monkeys hanging off the fronds and the row of totem poles I hand-goddam-crafted out of, I'm not kidding, foam-rubber kneepads. That year was the "Hawaiian Luau" birthday-party theme, complete with pig and poi, I swear. A friend finally intervened when I had an authentic Hawaiian dance troupe on the line, trying to negotiate them down from their thousand-dollar-plus fee. "Maybe you could cut the war dance but keep the fire-eating," she heard me say before she gently took the phone from my hand and said, simply, "Enough."

Ha! It was more than enough. It was over the top. I actually made thank-you notes, too, that featured a picture of Milly the morning after, sitting amidst a mountain of presents, ripped wrapping paper, shredded piñata, and the ankle-deep paste of trampled Polynesian food that covered everything. In it Milly is wearing red wooden shoes with her Powerpuff Girl pajamas, and the smile on her face is so radiant I just want to lean against a wall and clutch my chest.

I lost the list of who gave what, though, so I couldn't

send the note cards. This year I plan to use them as coasters, keeping a stack of them right there next to the steaming turkey legs and mutton, or whatever it is that medieval people eat, for chrissakes. This year it's a Renaissance theme, and I actually considered having a genuine jousting tournament, but realized I can't really fit horses in my house, not without risking some crushed kids, anyway.

"Kids got crushed all the time back then," Lary offers. "It would be authentic to the times."

Luckily Lary is good for other things. Like when I called him to say I wanted to make a castle in my house, he didn't even ask why. He just drove over here with a truck full of castle parts, or things that make great castle parts, and pretty soon I had one standing here, totally blocking my CD player on the bookshelf behind it. That's why Lary insists on the drawbridge. By that time other friends had arrived. "You need a dragon to go with the castle," one them said, and damn if one didn't materialize. It's every bit as big as the castle.

"You don't think it's over the top?" I ask them.

"Sometimes over the top is called for," they say, pouring themselves another glass of wine. By the time they left there was paint, glue, newspaper, gift wrap, and party supplies strewn about as if my house had been barfed on by a parade of giant birthday cakes, *and the party was still days away.*

I don't know where I inherited this neurotic-entertainer chromosome. Neither of my parents had it: the extent of their hospitality often only resulted in an open can of mixed nuts on the coffee table. My mother, in particular, was never one to go over the top for a houseguest. My brother once brought his college roommate home for dinner, an occasion for which my mother made a passable pan of canned-sauce lasagne with crumbled hamburger dotting the surface like gravel shaken from a shoe. Throughout the evening she was barefoot and wore one of my father's large button-down shirts over a pair of nylon shorts—or I'm assuming she was wearing shorts, anyway, as the shirt was long enough and the shorts short enough that the former completely camouflaged the latter, to the point that it seriously looked like my mother was serving us dinner in her underwear.

Looking back I'm very impressed with my brother's friend, who, if he was appalled to have the mother of his college roommate offer him dinner half naked, he didn't show it. He even asked for seconds, smiling when my mother, with smoldering menthol between her teeth, used a spatula to slap a slab on his plate.

You just never know about people. My father, for example, kept his usual place, standing in the corner of the kitchen where the counters met, and rolled his eyes at my mother. My sisters and I visibly died every other minute, so mortified we were that our mother looked like that floozie Michael Douglas just had casual sex with on *Streets of San Francisco*. But my brother's friend pretended not to notice us or my mother's bare feet and barely covered ass. He heaped compliments on my mother, who probably hadn't heard many lately, and he pretended to love that canned-sauce lasagne like it was flown in from Florence. It was a performance that was completely over the top, but sometimes over the top is called for.

LARY SAYS I NEED to start passing out in parking lots again. "I don't remember ever passing out in a parking lot," I tell him.

"That's just it," he says, "You used to be *wild*. You never remembered anything you did."

"Oh, Jesus God," I cry. "I'm not taking advice from some crazy goddam walking bag of body lice." And I did not even *ask* for the advice, mind you, yet here Lary is, pitching it out like manure patties.

It's not just him. Grant is sticking his huge head all up into my shit every chance he gets, too. "You need to fuck Matt," he tells me all the time. "Go fuck Matt."

"Let's count the reasons why that will never happen, okay?" I say. "One, he's *my friend*. Two, he used to *rob banks*! Three, he's, like, twenty-two, isn't he? Four, you've fucked him yourself five hundred times, right?"

Grant never answers that question, he just laughs. I have no idea what goes on between Matt and Grant, but I know something does. Anyway, Grant knows I would never, ever, ever, *ever* let him choose a man for me—not again, anyway—and that's what this is all about. These two complete crust pockets have decided that manlessness is my problem. I figure this must be because they are men themselves, in their own way, and as men they can't fathom not being needed.

Daniel doesn't really bother me about this. Don't forget that years ago on his endorsement I ended up dating a guy who fixes cars in his yard, and I've never let him forget that. Now he knows not to bolster my own awful taste in the opposite sex, and let's face it, my track record is a total toilet spin. I have absolutely no standards.

But goddam, I still feel lucky. I can't tell you how great it feels to open the door to my new home and know there's peace on the inside, as well as relative peace outside on the street. It's not the prettiest place to live, or the biggest, and the wallpaper in the bedroom will melt the retinas right out of your eye sockets, but at least it's mine. It's my reward for having no standards, and I'm okay with that.

Now I can't believe my friends want me to wreck everything all over again. Especially Lary. Lary loves his solitude like a smelly old troll. He doesn't even have a real door at his place, you just have to show up and holler outside his warehouse and hope he lets you in. That there is someone who does not want people in his life, believe me, yet here Lary is, giving me advice!

"Just what the hell am I gonna accomplish by passing out in a parking lot?" I ask.

"It's attractive," he says.

I bet it is. I bet an unconscious female attracts all kinds of crap. I wonder if that's how Lary finds the women he dates. If so, it's working pretty well for him. Lary usually dates women we're amazed would agree to be seen with him, though occasionally he throws a nutball into the mix, too, like the schizophrenic girl whose third personality is missing its left leg. She spent an entire afternoon once just hopping around out on the patio.

But still, Lary at least has standards. "I need a crazy-assed bitch in my life right now," was his standard then, and he met it.

Grant, for one, sees my lack of standards as a bonus. Grant came out of the closet at forty-two, and it must be great for a guy to figure out he's gay after a relative lifetime of heteroness, to discover this whole world of faceless sex free for the taking. I swear, I don't think there's a woman alive who will let you ass fuck her without at least a diamond bracelet in a box on the end table with her name on the card. Freshly gay, Grant found out there's a whole field of asses out there ripe for the fucking, and he does not even have to know their names or care whether they'd like him to. "I wonder why all men aren't gay," he says, knowing full well I know he thinks all men are.

I ask him if he remembers me ever passed out in a parking lot. "Girl, you were always passed out. Those were the good old days," he reminisces fondly. Right then I realize my friends don't know shit about what I need, but they are still my friends. They are the flotsam that got caught in the strainer of my life as the rest of the world flowed through. They are my reward for having no standards, and I'm okay with that.

FOR MONTHS NOW, Grant has been buying women's clothes, which by itself isn't anything new, but these women's clothes *don't fit him*. "Bitch," he said to me over the phone yesterday, "I just found the goddamnest, most gorgeous cocktail suit in fifties bubblegum blue. . . ."

"Bubblegum *blue*?" I asked.

"Believe me," he said, "when you see this blue suit, you will want to chew it. It's that fabulous."

I saw it, and he's right, it's that fabulous. "But it doesn't fit you," I pointed out.

"Whoreslutbitch," he said, exasperated, "I *know* that, do you not see me putting it into the special closet?"

That's right, Grant has a special closet. He's been keeping all the women's clothes that don't fit him in an entirely different closet from his own, one way down the hall. In addition to the cocktail suit, he has a blue Angie-Dickenson trench coat with contrast stitching, some sweater sets, two A-line shifts, a white patent-leather belt, and pantyhose.

I used to live in the Telephone Factory as well, in an apartment with the same floorplan just two doors down from where Grant lives now that he sold his shotgun shack in Peoplestown. I also used to use that closet for crap I was clinging to for odd reasons. Some of it didn't even belong to me, like the chipped plaster panther that my sister had unwisely given me for safekeeping eleven years ago. Evidently my mother had bought it for her in Tijuana, the world center for crap-ass plaster products. Why my sister thought it would be safer with me is a mystery, as it was chip-free when she handed it over. I also had a kitchen clock that once belonged to my grandmother. Besides a hand-knitted pincushion, that clock is the only heirloom I have.

"It doesn't even work," Grant said back then. He was always coming over to tell me I had to edit my possessions. "Divest yourself!" he'd holler. It could be heard echoing through the hallways. But I could not divest myself. I lugged that stuff through three addresses after that, and I still have it, though I seriously resent that panther. Now here's Grant with the same closet full of crap that's of no possible use to him, and I have to laugh. What *is* that in there? Is that a goddam pillbox hat?

"Divest yourself!" I holler at Grant. He's chasing me now because I've discovered that all that stuff in his special closet fits me fine, and I refuse to take off the blue Angie-Dickenson trench coat with contrast stitching. "God *damn* it, give that back, that is the one thing that fits me like a glove!" he shrieks.

Like hell it fits him. He was prancing around in it earlier, and his shoulders were about to bust through the back seam. "It's mine now and you know it," I taunt, and I can see he does know it. "Bitch," is all he says, but he's smiling as he shakes his head. The coat has banded sleeves with cuffs that turn up at the ends, and when I put it on, I just want to curl up in it, it's that wonderful.

In fact, everything in Grant's special closet is wonderful. The bubble-gum blue cocktail suit is a little tight in the hips, but hell, I could lose some more weight. It's been a while since I cared what I looked like, what with the kid, my absent love life, and the way I'd completely divested myself of any confidence regarding my ability to judge character. I was happy with my solitude, happy wearing the T-shirts and cargo pants and whatever else that stuck to me from the floor when I got up in the morning. I'd wad my hair on the top of my head like wet hay and hit the road. Nobody took notice of me, or at least I hope they didn't.

But Grant must have. When I met him eight years ago I was living in that same building, and I used to wear white high-heeled sandals and a sundress you could fit into an envelope. Sometimes

I'd take my tennis racket and whack balls against the brick wall of the Turner building next door. Once Grant walked over and leaned against the wall I was whacking, and I remember thinking he had a lot of confidence in me, because one wrong shot and he'd lose an eye, I swear. But he leaned there and talked to me anyway, and I didn't hit him.

Back then Grant was heavy, bald, and clad in overalls, but that is not the most surprising part. The most surprising part is that he was not gay. He was stuffed way back in the closet, on the tail end of his second marriage, and after ten careers, three kids, and seven redecorated living rooms, Grant had not yet found himself. For some reason our friendship emerged as part of the path that helped him get there.

Since then, my own path has proven to have had some surprising forks. Motherhood, for one, was a complete bolt from the blue, and through it all I worried I'd lose my friends, because people fall from you when you change, they drift away like dead leaves. But I did not lose my friends. What I had lost was myself— that is, until Grant opened his special closet, and there I was again.

GRANT IS SO AFRAID I'm gonna find Jesus that he sometimes reminds me of my atheist mother, who used to fend off Bible-wielding Jesus freaks with lit cigarettes. He's downright protective, Grant is, whenever someone tries to save my soul, whereas personally I'm pretty flattered by the effort, such as this most recent attempt by a lady at the American Thrift store.

"That lady with the jacket just saved my soul," I told him, skipping through an aisle of old prom dresses. "I'm going to heaven," I singsonged, "while your freckled fag ass is gonna fry in hell. Ha, ha."

"Goddamit! Where is that bitch?" he bitched, his eyes searching the store for her. "I'm gonna tell her God told me she needs to tithe that jacket to you."

He was talking about the vintage jacket the lady had snagged right out from under his nose, which was pretty swift, I must admit. It's hard to out-thrift Grant. He'd already found me the dress that went with the jacket, a short-sleeved shift from the '60s made from an awesome aqua-colored, puckered polyester, and he could see the matching jacket from four aisles away. He was headed there like a hornet, believe me, but the lady got there before him.

Grant asked her to give it up, which would never have occurred to me to do. He is the master, I tell you. She said no, nicely, so I told Grant I planned to offer her the dress, since it would be a shame to split a matching set. "Are you crazy?" he hissed at me under his breath so she wouldn't hear. "Don't you dare give it up! I will *kill* you." But I asked her if she wanted it anyway, and she declined. Grant sighed with relief and ambled off to look at some '70s leisure suits that appeared to be made from lightweight sofa upholstery.

After he left, the lady apologized for wanting to keep the jacket, and even offered to help me find me another one that might look just as good, or maybe a white crocheted vest such as the one she just found, which was long and something Bea Arthur would have worn on *Maude*. But I was happy with the dress just as it was, and happy too that the matching jacket wasn't wasted on someone who didn't appreciate it, and that is when the lady saved my soul.

"I feel there's a reason God gave us each a piece of a matching set today," she began, "so I just have to ask, have you given your heart to Jesus?"

Before I go any further, let me just say that, when I was a kid, I used to be frightened by fervor. When we lived in Melbourne, Florida, my mother often threatened to forsake her atheism just so she could have me carted to a Christian boot camp called "The Seed," where unruly kids were deposited for months at a stretch, during which time their surliness was somehow psychologically beaten out of them. Even the coolest of kids came out vapid faced with fervor. Even slutty Wendy, who had curly mermaid hair to her waist and used to wear her jeans so low and loose that you could practically see her pubes when she thrust her hand in her front pocket for a pack of cigarettes, even she came out with her hair cut off and her collar buttoned up.

That was a surprise, let me tell you. None of us thought Wendy would give up her surliness. It had us all petrified that The Seed had some special power that could suck all the fun out of people. Afterward, Wendy always sat alone at the front of the school bus, where the rest of us stared at her with the curiosity of aliens itching to probe a bovine. She tried to save a few souls, mine included, asking us if we'd given our hearts to Jesus. I said I had, which is kind of true, because when I was seven I'd been allowed to attend church with a friend, and I'd approached the podium when the preacher called forth sinners from the audience. I asked Jesus into my heart then, though I was unconvinced he'd hang around for long.

When I told Wendy that, she asked if I'd sit beside her, so I did. The whole time she tried to resave my soul, and I got the feeling it was less for my sake than for hers, like she was worried she'd be the only one on the bus going to heaven. After that I was a little less afraid of fervor, because I could see in Wendy's eyes that I was mistaking fervor for something else. The lady at American Thrift had eyes like that, and I figured if saving my soul saved her from a few more moments of loneliness then I was happy to give it up for a bit.

God, was Grant pissed. "Where is that bitch?" he kept saying, like he was gonna chase her down and get her to give it back. I had to laugh. "You're going to hell alone," I taunted him, knowing full well that if anyone can make a heaven of hell, it's Grant. He spotted the lady walking out the door, but I held him back and off she walked with my soul, just one piece of a matching set, snagged like a vintage jacket right out from under Grant's nose.

I THOUGHT BEGGING WAS behind me. For example, there's that particular panhandler who has staked out the freeway on-ramp where I used to live. He shuffles around, dragging tatters behind him and sporting a ragged cardboard sign that says, "Hungry. Homeless. Help Me. God Bless." The words are scratched out weakly, like those you'd find on the underside of a coffin lid of somebody buried alive. In fact, the beggar very much reminds me of a mummy, not the kind preserved with meticulous ceremony, but the kind you find in peat bogs by accident thousands of years after they died there, snake bitten.

"He's a superb specimen," I say to myself in a scientist's accent every time the beggar limps near to peer into my car window. His remaining teeth are the color of old mustard, his eyes are vacuous, his stature is bent, defeated, and his skin is stretched across his bones like dried hide. He truly looks like he's rotting right before my eyes.

It's a great act, and I'd fall for it if I hadn't seen the other side of him. When a cop car pulls up, the cultivated deadness in the beggar's demeanor disappears at once. In fact, he brightens like a birthday candle as he beats a hasty escape, darting between the cars with the agility of a basketball player. Oh, so that's what this is, I realized when I first saw him do that, all this begging is just his *gig*.

Some people are good at it, I guess. Not me. I tried panhandling as a child, after accidentally hitting pay dirt one day while loitering at a department store with my sisters. Earlier that morning we'd discovered a mud pool inside a massive concrete pipe abandoned by city workers, and we'd played waist deep in it all day, and I suppose we looked so pathetic that a woman felt compelled to compensate us for it, bestowing a dollar in my palm like the touch of a wand.

This is *great,* I glowed, figuring I'd found my life's vocation. So for the next few days I moped pitifully about in public places, projecting, in my mind, such a convincing image of sadness and deprivation that more money would surely fly at me from people's wallets like foam from a can of shaken Shasta. I tried to exude the weight of the ages on my tiny shoulders, and audibly sighed so often I got dizzy from hyperventilation. None of this garnered a single additional dime, though, so eventually I had to go back to selling cupcakes door to door.

So you'd think that lesson would have seared itself into my psyche after that, but remarkably that wasn't the last time I'd fail at begging. Later there'd be that boy in high school I'd foolishly fall in love with, the one who moved to Australia. I placed the future of my minuscule universe on the cusp of his upturned mouth, hoping to attach myself to the fleeting coattails of all of his hopes and dreams, of which he had many.

But sadly I'd been relegated to part of the small-time trap he ached to escape, so he drove me home one night and, fairly unceremoniously, proceeded to dump me like a load of toxic waste. I *begged* him, with heaving sobs, to take me with him, but my groveling only strengthened his resolve, as it should have, I suppose. I don't remember if he had to physically pull me out of his car or what, but looking back at my absence of dignity, I don't see how else I would have left. So he must have pulled me out, yes, and then pulled away. In every sense pulled away. Watching him leave, one lucid thought bubbled to my brain as I stood on the curbside blubbering: "I bet the begging," I berated myself sardonically, "was a real turn-on."

So like I said, I thought begging was behind me. I would rather die than beg, I've thought lots of times in the past decade. But lately that conviction has begun to crumble, mostly because of what I've read lately. Take the deputy who was shot by Al-Amin, the cop-killing Muslim cleric who is now serving life without possibility of parole. I read the deputy begged Al-Amin to let him live. He lay there on the asphalt, begging for his life. I think of that and realize my own arrogance. *Rather die than beg?* If it were me, with my life in someone else's palm, put there by evil or other circumstances, teetering on being dismissed with one gassy-assed breath from my abductor, it would take me less than a second to assess the lovely shit basket that has become my life—the struggles, the failings, the loves both lost and found, the dreams both broken and not so broken, the tiny toehold of happiness I've finally managed to carve out for myself. It would take me less than a second, I tell you, and I would be begging.

LUCKY YATES AND ANNA ARE DATING. *Each other*. After all the blustering they both did about how they'd grown a sturdy layer of rust around their emotions, how they were never again gonna get tricked into the yawning butt-hole of bad love by letting that layer soften a little, they both crumbled like stale coffee cake the second they had some alone-time together. Ha! How's that for conviction?

"We made out for, like, ninety minutes in my car," Anna said, not even a little ashamed.

"Bitch, you two were supposed to be my comrades in crusty solitude," I laugh. I'd introduced them awhile ago, after listening to them both blather about newfound backbone due to their respective freshly failed relationships, and how this was supposed to serve as a force field against future sentimental involvement of any kind. They each sounded about as convincing as a recovering alcoholic hanging out at Hooters on free-beer night, so I thought they'd get along.

On the other hand, of course, if they end up hating each other I deny any responsibility. Just like I deny any responsibility for unleashing Lary into the world. Lary would have been here regardless. I swear I did not create him. He came out demented the minute he was born, an event I don't think even involved an actual mammal—just magma, maybe, coming from a crack in the earth's core. I figure this is the reason for his famous fascination with Cheez Whiz. Maybe it reminds him of the primordial ooze from which he first crawled.

"Did you know they sell Cheez Whiz by the gallon?" he asked me the other day, and damn if he did not have a *gallon* of Cheez Whiz sitting right there on the bar stool next to him. Cheez Whiz of that mass doesn't come in a plastic jug like you might think, but a metal drum similar to the kind they use for commercial solvents. He says he stole it from the Omni Hotel, off the set of a cooking show hosted by Emeril Lagasse, who "was really hungover," according to Lary. I have a hard time believing a famous chef would need an industrial drum of Cheez Whiz, but then maybe he kept it around for the curiosity factor, because the sight of it really is a little mesmerizing. Cheez Whiz is like earwax, and not just in the obvious sense, but because you're only accustomed to encountering it in tiny amounts.

Lary has looked into making his own, and swears the process is a heralded scientific achievement. "I always thought it would be like Superman squeezing coal into a diamond, but it's not," he says excitedly. "It's a subatomic reaction. It's what the Iraqis were working on before we invaded."

I swear I thought he was gonna start sleeping with that stuff, so I was surprised to hear he'd offered it to Grant to augment the appetizer buffet at his upcoming Sister Louisa art exhibit, titled "The Third Coming." Everyone will be there: me, Lucky Yates, Anna, Lary, Daniel, and the rest of the psycho circus—which reminds me, Grant better step up on the grub. The last Sister Louisa art exhibit I attended featured cheese puffs, cut-up Krispy Kreme doughnuts, and bad wine in a box, which Grant himself hauled around and squirted into people's cups. Amazingly, he still wonders why all his potted plants were dead within a week.

But this time Grant promises the drum of Cheez Whiz is just for display. He probably won't even open it. "Besides," he sniffs, "this is not about feeding your body, it's about feeding your *brain*."

I would laugh if not for the fact that, amazingly, people really do tend to derive emotional nourishment from Sister Louisa's trailer-vangelical wisdom, which is painted on societal discards, such as the cracked mirror graced with the statement, *Celebrate the flaw*.

I love looking in that mirror. I don't just see me, but the entire carnival that comprises my friends and family. We are all flawed in the most fabulous ways.

Take Lary, who seriously cannot recall how a complicated network of scaffolding came to be erected in his kitchen, or how that truck bed ended up on the roof of his house. "I just know it was harder to get down than it was to get up," is all he offers. Or Daniel, who spends his days at a mental hospital, not as a patient but as a care provider who teaches art to troubled children every day, a process that will suck the human faith out of anyone else. But somehow he manages to emerge with most of himself in tow, the pieces having been left behind with the hope of future retrieval. Then there is Lucky Yates and Anna, two emotional refugees whose hearts were used as total toilet paper in the past, but who nonetheless decided to test their toes in the same tub again. Christ, you have got to commend them for that, right? However it turns out, at least they were brave enough to try. At least there is that to say about all of us. Rather than turn away, we decide to look into the mirror, see past the cracks, and celebrate the flaws.

THIS PAGE IS DEDICATED TO the people who believed in me, because if not for them, I might just be living in Lary's truck right now, which still does not even have a front seat.

First, I want to thank my mother and father for not being perfect. In fact, if I were magically granted just one minute with them again, I'd tell them I love the person (and the mother) those imperfections caused me to become.

Then there is the rest of my family (which is by far not isolated to people who share my parents); my sister Kim and her husband Eddie, my other sister Cheryl, my brother Jim and his wife Cindy, my alleged stepfather Bill (who is also allegedly dead), and, of course, Daniel Troppy, Grant Henry, and Lary Blodgett, with a special thanks to the dear Daniel Keiger, who, among the many reasons he earned my gratitude, flat out refused to hire me as a bartender.

My daughter deserves my ultimate appreciation, as there is no greater catapult for self-improvement than the simple adoration bestowed on you from your child's eyes, and the need to live up to it. Also, I want to emphasize that my daughter is not fatherless. On the contrary, she is very much loved and cared for in this regard.

Also, I owe an ocean of gratitude to my editors at *Creative Loafing*: Suzanne Van Atten, Jim Stawniak, Ken Edelstein, and Doug Monroe, as well as the staff and other writers there for producing a paper that surrounds my column with such quality. I also want to thank (again!) Patrick Best, Steve Hedberg, and Rebecca Burns, who were all there at the very beginning when my column was just an ember, fanning it so it wouldn't die out. Damn am I grateful to them for that.

And thank God for Jay Leno, Jolie Ancel, Michele Conklin, Mike Henry, Jill Hannity, Judith Regan, Cassie Jones, Tammi Guthrie, Neal Boortz, and my producer at NPR's *All Things Considered*, Sarah Sarasohn.

The following people also remain in my gratitude: Liz Lapidus, Josh Levs, Kathy Jett, Jesse Chamberlin, Sherrie Cash, Matt Barrineau, Marcia Wood, Tom Junod, Karyn Slaughter, Jim Hackler, Mary Rose Kelly, Julie Bookman, Michael Benoit, Teresia Mosher, Sarah Rosenberg, Lynn Lamousin, Corinne Lynch, Laura Geraci, Thomas Meagher, Nena Halford, Gina Speakmon, Jim Llewellyn, Anna Llewellyn, Lucky Yates, Bob and Lu Steed, Corinne Lynch, Michael Alvear, Randy Osborne, Polly Sheppard, Samuel Johnson, and, most importantly, the readers of my columns and books and my listeners on NPR.

Lastly, I'm so very thankful to my former neighbors of Capitol View, among them Miss Taylor, Monty and Greta DeMayo, Muggs DeMayo, and especially Todd Kitchens, Honnie Goode, and her mother Bren. Their grace and dignity beautified the surroundings in a way that resonates to this day. Today the place is downright lovely.